"My friend Nicole Crank makes your dream doable. In her book *Goal Getters: 5 Steps to Finally Getting What You Want* she lays out the five steps to your destiny. Don't let your history define your horizons. Nicole will tell you stories with great candor and transparency. You will be challenged, excited and certainly motivated to take the five steps to success."

—Sam Chand, Leadership Consultant and author of *Harnessing the Power of Tension* (www.samchand.com)

"If you don't make goals for yourself you have nothing to shoot for. Having the attitude of just playing the game isn't my strength. I have to be productive. That's my responsibility. *Goal Getters* can put you on the right track to success."

—Jim Edmonds, Retired St. Louis Cardinals Centerfielder Winner 8 Gold Gloves, 4 Time All Star, 6 Time League MVP

"Now more than ever, people need clarity and purpose. Nicole's newest book, *Goal Getters*, is more than a good book, it's a roadmap for everyone to maximize their potential. Nicole lays out, beautifully, everything you need in a simple yet profound new way. All you need to do is follow it! No matter where you are in life, to be successful we have to keep growing...*Goal Getters* is a life changing resource to ensure you don't get off course."

—Lee Domingue, Author-*Pearls of the King & The Family Meeting Guide* Founder-Kingdom Builders U.S. and Trafficking Hope, CEO-m360, L.L.C.

"It's rare to find a goal strategy that includes a constant look to our Heavenly Father. I love how Nicole is attacking her days with passion and fervor, all the while keeping her perspective anchored in Jesus. That's what all life-giving leaders need!"

—Tyler Reagin, Founder of the Life-Giving Company, Author of *Leading Things You Didn't Start*, former President of Catalyst

"Pastor Nicole Crank takes on the challenge of improving one's life with great faith in the human spirit, wisdom that comes with her uniquely vast experience, and lots of humor. Her book is a solid testimony as to our societal need to see more women, like Pastor Crank in public, civic, an political leadership positions. Crank's message – that what keeps us away from the life we want can be effectively addressed and even fixed – is empowering and inspiring, at the same time. I strongly recommend picking up this book as a first step on a journey empowered by faith and guided by fate."

—Ido Aharoni Aronoff, Global Ambassador Genius 100 Visions

"Pastor Nicole has a special anointing for giving you the one-two-punch in her writing, with both the love of God, and the hook of the truth that will set you free. I'm so honored to know someone who isn't afraid to "go there" with all of the important topics most Christians "won't," "shouldn't," or just don't talk about. This book will help you get down to brass tacks in not just goal-setting, but as Nicole says: 'Goal-Getting!'"

—Megan Swanson, Miss Nebraska USA 2020,
Miss Nebraska (America) 2014, CEO & Founder,
Powerhouse Pageantry, Speaker and Singer/Songwriter

"It's easy to get sucked into a vortex of boredom when you don't have a clear picture of where you're headed in life. Even if you have a dream in sight, it's easy to get overwhelmed if you don't have manageable steps, or someone to guide you along the way. We need goals—both natural and spiritual. Without them, life can easily overwhelm us. Nicole Crank's new book, *Goal Getters*, provides a roadmap to help you set and reach obtainable goals and not get overwhelmed in the process. God has hardwired his children to pursue the best for their lives, but we need people like Nicole to help us along the way to successfully achieve those goals. In this insightful book, Nicole provides the reader with a meaningful and manageable picture of your future, based on God's word, personal stories, along with insightful and practical steps to get the upmost out of one's life. Reading *Goal Getters*, will help you become the person you were destined to be."

—Marcus D. Lamb, Founder-President
Daystar Television Network

GOAL GETTERS

5 Steps to Finally Getting What You Want

NICOLE CRANK

AVAIL

Scripture quotations marked KJV are taken from the King James Version of the Bible. Public domain. Scripture quotations marked NIV are taken from the Holy Bible, New International Version®, NIV®. Copyright © 1973, 1978, 1984, 2011 by Biblica, Inc.™ Used by permission of Zondervan. All rights reserved worldwide. www.zondervan. com. The "NIV" and "New International Version" are trademarks registered in the United States Patent and Trademark Office by Biblica, Inc.™ | Scripture quotations marked NKJV are taken from the New King James Version®. Copyright © 1982 by Thomas Nelson. Used by permission. All rights reserved. | Scripture quotations marked TLB are taken from The Living Bible Copyright © 1971 by Tyndale House Foundation. Used by permission of Tyndale House Publishers Inc., Carol Stream, Illinois 60188. All rights reserved. The Living Bible, TLB, and The Living Bible logo are registered trademarks of Tyndale House Publishers. | Scripture quotations marked NLT are taken from the *Holy Bible*, New Living Translation, copyright © 1996, 2004, 2015 by Tyndale House Foundation. Used by permission of Tyndale House Publishers, Inc., Carol Stream, Illinois 60188. All rights reserved. | Scripture quotations marked MSG are taken from *THE MESSAGE*, copyright © 1993, 1994, 1995, 1996, 2000, 2001, 2002 by Eugene H. Peterson. Used by permission of NavPress. All rights reserved. Represented by Tyndale House Publishers, Inc. | Scripture quotations marked GNT are from the Good News Translation in Today's English Version— Second Edition. Copyright © 1992 by American Bible Society. Used by Permission. Scripture quotations marked AMP taken from The Amplified Bible®, Copyright © 1960, 1962, 1963, 1968, 1971, 1972, 1973, 1975, 1977, 1995 by The Lockman Foundation. Used by permission. www.Lockman.org.

For foreign and subsidiary rights, contact the author.

Cover design by: Joe DeLeon
Cover photo by: Chosen Photography

ISBN: 978-1-950718-68-9   1 2 3 4 5 6 7 8 9 10

Printed in the United States of America

Contents

Getting Ready

STEAK, BONES, AND HOT DOGS: GETTING YOUR DREAM CAPACITY READY

I have a 2.2-pound Yorkie named Luppy. You think I'm tough, don't you? Don't prejudge…

We've had her for over a decade. The day she came home with us as a Christmas gift, she fit entirely in the palm of my hand. She is the smallest dog I've ever seen—almost half the size of our giant, 3.8-pound Pomeranian (yeah, not helping my tough image). Let's be honest: if anyone tries to break into our house, those two dogs aren't going to stop them. Unless…

Unless there's food involved. If you put a steak bone on the floor, Luppy develops this thing our family has come to call "rat eyes." There's a look she gets that is straight up primal, and she'll do her best to tear your hand right off your body if you DARE to reach for that bone! I'm serious. She can do some damage!

We have high regard for the amount of fierce determination in that little fur ball.

She isn't aware of her size at that moment and isn't about to let that stop her from getting what she wants. We all know dogs like bones. That's why she fights so hard... *Or is it?*

DO DOGS REALLY LIKE BONES?

Honestly, no. They don't. Dogs like steak, but we just give them the bones. If Luppy could turn the tables with those big eyes—eyes that can turn vicious in a flash at the opportunity for a *bone*—she would keep the steak and give *me* the bone. She would treat me like a dog! She would finally get what she wanted.

That's what I feel like a lot of us are doing: we're just living on the *bones* of life. We've been settling for the leftovers. We've been surviving on just the scraps that come our way. Today, I want to encourage you. You're not living a "scraps" kind of life anymore. Only occasionally wishing for that "steak" life where we see a happy family, our dream house, the car that looks like it's fueled by fun instead of gasoline, or someone else's vacation pictures.

We all hunger for the steak life. We see it, but we don't exactly know how to grab hold of it. That changes *now*. We're not going to set bare bones kind of goals. We're going to set steak goals and we're going to eat off the table God has prepared for us!

I know that puppy love leads to a dog's life! But the Bible says that even the dogs get the crumbs that fall from the table (Matthew 15:27). But friend, you ain't no dog! (Bad grammar to emphasize a statement that's meant to shake you out of your small-thinking mindset.) You are so much more!

ABOVE ALL YOU CAN IMAGINE

I remember more than ten years ago, when we were looking for a building for our second church campus. My husband and I pastor a church in two states with six locations. Today, it looks like we know how to do multi-site/multi-state church campuses in our sleep. But this was our very first expansion location. Back in December of 2007 we didn't know that anyone else was even doing this!

We were looking around, just building shopping. (Let me be more honest: we were building *dreaming*. We didn't know how we were going to afford this move.) We looked at a 125,000-square-foot building that had been assessed for over $19 *million* dollars. It used to be a Sam's Club and had since been redesigned to be a conference center.

The building had been completely remodeled with the finest finishes: marble, cherry wood, stainless steel bathrooms, auto-everything, new air conditioning units, paint… it was so in style! The business had been foreclosed on, and the bank was asking $6.3 million dollars for it.

We had no idea how to make the payment on that much of a loan, even though most of the work had already been done. So, we did what any sensible pastors would do: we looked for something more affordable. Just one mile away lay our Ishmael: a K-mart that had been abandoned for over a decade. It needed *everything*! When it rained outside, it rained *inside* and left puddles. The air conditioning didn't work, and I'm pretty sure everything was covered in mold. But the parking lot was big (although it needed to be entirely repaved). They were only asking $4 million dollars. That seemed so much more affordable to us. We would still need millions more for the remodel, but we would have time to acquire the money.

We took our leadership team to look at both buildings. The nice building already had a contract on it and wasn't even available. We were just dreaming and considering what was possible. We talked about how we couldn't possibly afford this amazing building (the company that had been foreclosed on had spent another $14 million remodeling it, on top of the amazing features already there). *Oh well*, we thought. *Perhaps, the other building wouldn't look so bad in the end.* One of our longtime leaders looked at David and me and said,

*"I don't think God would show you a steak
and then give you a hot dog."*

We laughed and went on with our day. A couple of weeks later, the bank called. The other contract couldn't get the financing necessary to close on the nice building. If we could get a financial letter of commitment from the bank in two weeks, and go hard on the contract, the building could be ours. We crunched the numbers every way we knew how but always came up with the same answer: We didn't know if we could afford steak. We'd always been hot dog people.

Friend, you can't forget this fact: you serve a God who is exceedingly, abundantly above all you can *ask* (I have a big "ask" capacity), *think* (I think constantly), or *imagine* (and baby, I've got let's-go-to-the-moon-sized dreams)! Faith doesn't even begin until our ability ends (a quote from my book, *Hi God, It's Me Again*) and without faith, it's *impossible* to please God.

All that faith-stretching Bible truth to emphasize this: staying at home with a small dream doesn't make God happy (and it shouldn't make you happy). He wants you out there trying to walk on water. If you'll attempt what seems impossible in your own strength and step out in faith, there won't be any bones for you. No hot dogs. There will be *steak*.

On the very last day of our two-week deadline, the bank called and told us they would give us the financing. We fell to the ground in our home and cried and shouted and laughed and cried some more.

And the rest is history!

NO MORE HOT DOGS

You might not know how to take your first bite of steak. I'm here to help guide you, step-by-step, from "I don't even know what my dream is" to actually checking off those goal boxes... *in the next twelve months.*

You might have tried before and failed. That's great! Now you know what *not* to do. I'm here to explain some of those failures and give you methods, tips, tricks and encouragement to succeed this time. You might have gotten bored, distracted or veered off course. I'm going to show you methods and offer you tools to get rid of your dream-stealers.

And my favorite: you might think you're unworthy—"Someone like me couldn't possibly..." You're talking to a girl who lived a third of her life on a gravel road. *Hello, backwoods country!* On top of that, I was adopted; I was born in another country; I was raped; I was molested; I was a victim of spousal physical, mental and emotional abuse from my crack-addicted ex-husband.

Yet, somehow, God saw fit to use somebody "like me." He uses the foolish things of the world to confound the wise (1 Corinthians 1:27). This can be your scripture too, if you want. I figured that, if a donkey in the Bible can talk, so can I. God can use anybody He wants to use. It *delights* Him when you do things you could never do on your own. That way, we don't get the credit—we're forced to give it all to Him!

Live little, and you'll stay exactly where the enemy wants you to be. You have unseen forces trying to keep you from dreaming today. We're going to release those dreams and, more than that, we're going to give you five steps to finally getting what you want: the "Get It" Method.

FIVE SIMPLE STEPS

These steps aren't just to help you dream again—they're to help you enter into the dream that God planted in your heart. It's not just yours. God planted it in your heart and here I am today, trying to pull it out. These five steps are so clear and easy that even an elementary school student could pull them off without much trouble.

You're going to *set*—and actually *get*—your goals.

- I can't wait for you to *get* a Vision.
- We'll architect an action plan to help you *get* Going.

- I'll show you the way to *get* Results, as we stay committed, and you start achieving more than you ever have before!
- And—my favorite part, and the most often-overlooked part—we'll take time to *get* Happy and celebrate the little wins on the way to your dream.

This program isn't hard. In fact, it's remarkably easy!

I'm going to prove to you, using science, that you need to be making plans to live a different kind of life next year. If you work this program, you're going to be a real Goal-Getter!

God wants to release your potential.

The Lord Almighty is beckoning you to fulfill your purpose.
My Father and my Redeemer is asking you to step up.
The Creator of the Universe is praying for you to say *yes*.
God is looking to and fro on the earth for someone to bless.

SAY THIS: (out loud, you have to be committed)

That. Is. Me.
I am open.
I am teachable.
I embrace change.
I can dream big.
There *is* more for me.
I will believe for it.

I will pursue it.
I will walk in it.
And I start *today!*

BLESSING YOUR DREAM

Father God,

In the name of Jesus, I pray over my friends. Jeremiah 29:11 says "I know the plans I have for you. They're for good, and not for evil: to bring you to an expected end, to bring you a future and a hope." The Bible says, "Before you were in the womb, I knew you and I had a plan for you. I called you to be a prophet to the nations".

God, I pray for the call on each and every one of these readers—I pray that they hear the sound of Your voice in their own hearts, right now. We're pulling the dream out of them. Thank you, God, for connecting us today. Thank you, God, for the ability to dream again!

So here's the deal: I'm spiritual, *but* I am going to push you like a college football coach and cheer for you like the Dallas Cowboy Cheerleaders (my fave team since I was little).

Are you ready to stop living on bones?
Does steak sound good (metaphorically, for my vegan friends)?

Are you ready to stop *setting* goals and start *getting* goals?
Are you ready to get your dreams off paper and into reality?
Then grab your pen and paper, put aside those hot-dog
thoughts, and turn the page. There's no time like the present.

Let's *go to work!*

Step One:

SET IT AND GET IT: DREAMING AND SETTING YOUR GOALS

START WITH THIS...

I need you to ask one question as we begin. Write down your answer, maybe even in your Goal-Getters Study Guide or Planner, because *clarity of vision brings clarity of life*. So here's your question:

What would it take for this year to be the most amazing year of your life?

Would it take starting your business? Is it having the baby you've been wanting? Maybe it's paying off your house and living mortgage-free? What about getting that next promotion? Would it take paying off your credit cards? Or is your dream buying a car? How about meeting the person you've been hoping for? Maybe it's finally writing the book, or even being financially free to help people around the world?

What would it take for this year to be the most amazing year of your life? That's the question we're going to answer with our goals.

We begin by asking ourselves that question and writing down our dreams. Then we take a step that makes certain we aren't wasting our time heading in the wrong direction: we stop and pray. We take the time—right now, as soon as we jot down our dreams—to consult the wisest Being that ever was. We seek the One who knows the beginning from the end—the God who created us for a purpose and a pursuit. Man has his plans. We can come up with whatever we want; but God directs our steps.

Do you ever feel like you're just wandering around in life, stumbling into a great opportunity by accident? Or maybe you feel like you're wasting a lot of time and effort on projects that you're stoked about for a couple of weeks or months, but then end up half-written in a box or a Google Drive file somewhere. I do. Seriously. Believe it or not, everybody feels that way! It seems like, no matter how well-planned we think we are in our business pursuits and our life in general, we all veer off the road of destiny just a little.

Are you a good driver? I know you think you are. We all *think* we're good drivers… including that guy who's updating his Facebook status as he speeds down the highway at 65 miles per hour, swerving like he's had one too many. It's easy to throw shade at him. But as we're driving, answering our cell phones, changing the radio station and drinking our coffees, we honk, we yell, "Stupid driver!" at that poor gent who almost hit us on the highway by getting distracted out of his lane... and now we're doing the same thing!

We All Wander off the Path a Little Bit

It's God's voice that will keep us on the direct path to our destiny and His blessing. But His path is not always what we think it is.

> *"For my thoughts are not your thoughts, neither are your ways my ways," declares the Lord. "As the heavens are higher than the earth, so are my ways higher than your ways and my thoughts than your thoughts."*
> —Isaiah 55:8-9 (NIV)

We don't think like God thinks. We don't have ideas like God has ideas. God can see the end of a thing from the beginning. We're not rewarded for our intentions; we're rewarded for our completions. God is ready for us to get some stuff *done*!

> *"If we are preparing without involving God, we may be preparing for the wrong things."*
> —from *Hi God, One More Thing*

We need to insert God into every part of our plan. "Every part" includes examining where we are, identifying our goals and making plans on how we're going to get there. Then, we need to prayerfully plan along with what God has called us to do.

> *"Listen for God's voice in everything you do, everywhere you go; He's the one who will keep you on track (or path)."*
> —Proverbs 3:6 (MSG)

We need to say, "Okay God, here's what I want to do. What do You think?" We're going to check with Him and make sure it's what He wants us to do by praying for peace or disruption in our heart. Why? It's not just that you'll spin your wheels and get nowhere; outside of God's will for your life, there's leprosy. If you're not sure about that, just ask Gehazi. That's how he got it.

Gehazi had a plan to make himself big *outside of his call*. He wanted to be Elisha, the chief, in charge. Instead, he was number two on the totem pole. He was being groomed for greatness, but it wasn't coming fast enough for him. So he lied about who he was and what he was doing and got what he *thought* he wanted.

Elisha had just met with another man who had offered him gifts. Elisha didn't accept anything from him, but Gehazi wanted his proverbial Armani suit. Without Elisha's consent, Gehazi chased after the man, got clothes and money and slipped into his Fifth Avenue duds. He put on the clothes of the leper that he should've never received in the first place.

The leprosy was in the clothes that he put on, and he got contaminated. (Check out 2 Kings 5:20-27 to read more about it.)

There's leprosy outside of your call. God never says "no" to keep you from something unless it's something He knows is *not good for you*.

So we asked one question: *What would it take for this to be the most amazing year of my life?* Then, we have to check with God. Only then can we start writing down our goals.

WRITE THIS DOWN

Clarity of vision brings clarity of life.

I'm going to ask you to write some things down while you're reading this book.

I always say that the shortest pencil is better than the longest memory. I heard a statistic that says if we don't write down a thought, within 37 seconds we lose it to the door bell, the text message, the squirrel, the dryer buzzer, the interruption... you get it. Research on the forgetting curve shows that, within *one hour*—60 little minutes—people forget an average of 50 percent of the information they just received. Within 24 hours, they forget an average of 70 percent of new information. Within a week, usually 90 percent of new information is gone *forever*. Don't waste your time! It's your most precious commodity.[1]

---

1. Kohn, "Brain Science: The Forgetting Curve–the Dirty Secret of Corporate Training," Learning Solutions, *https://learningsolutionsmag.com/articles/1379/brain-science-the-forgetting-curvethe-dirty-secret-of-corporate-training*

So, for real, *never* read an exercise and say, "I'll do that later." No, you won't. Clarity of vision brings clarity of life. So let's *get clear* and write it down.

Where do you write? That's the next hurdle, right? Get prepared. I suggest the *Goal Getters Study Guide or Planner*. I have some resources on my website you can download for free at *NicoleCrank.com*. At the very least, grab a notebook or write in the margins of this book. Today we're doing things a little differently: a marginal change for a maximum gain.

This book isn't passive, it's active. Read, pause, write. Don't rush the process. Why? Because I'm taking you somewhere, regardless of where you've been. Your past doesn't determine your future. Don't think about last year—that chapter's closed. Don't think about last month—we've turned the page on that. That thing that they said about you, the self-imposed limit you've slapped on yourself, that anchor that's trying to hold you down?

No, no, no. That's over today.

The Top 3%

Well, what's so significant about today? *This* is the day that you're making a commitment to write down your goals and to head toward your future. Let me share a fact that will floor you:

In a study done by Dr. Gale Matthews, Dr. Matthews found that *just writing down your goals gives you a 42% higher chance of reaching your goal.*

It only takes writing them down to be almost halfway there! So grab that paper and pen. Don't just get your computer out. Forage for writing supplies, if you have to! The process of writing is actually a mental commitment to making it happen.

We aren't just going to write our goals—we're going to *get* them. And don't worry, I'm going to help you know *exactly* what to write and how to write them so you'll get there. You know you're going to *get* there, right? You're not like you used to be.

The truths shared in this book aren't hard or even time consuming. They're little tweaks that lead to giant peaks. Peaks that will take you to the top. And you're headed there right now. Did you know that 97% of Americans don't write down any goals? You can get ahead of 97% of the people in the world by committing your goals to paper. By that one simple act, you enter the top 3% of people! Congratulations, you're about to enter an upper echelon already.

Harvard Business School did a study on some of their students. (Don't tune out just because you didn't go to an Ivy League school. I didn't go to Harvard either! We have something in common, right? Most of us are just glad we graduated high school at all! LOL. I'm feeling you.) The university studied them all the way through school and for years into their careers.

At the end of the study, they recorded some pretty phenomenal separators. The top three alumni in the study in terms of power, influence, and highest financial gain all had *one* thing in common: they had written goals. The rest of the Harvard graduates hadn't kept up with their success—none of them had bothered to write goals in the first place! Even their Ivy League education didn't give them the same edge that taking the time and focus to write their goals did.

You might be thinking,

Uh, but remember, I didn't go to Harvard at all!

God doesn't want you to get stuck where you started. Your zip code, education—or lack thereof—doesn't determine your future. You are here on purpose. You were created for a reason. God just needed you on this earth so He could use you to fulfill the destiny He has for you. God didn't create no junk (bad grammar, good theology). He made you, and He's got an idea for where He wants you to go. We've simply had some things that have kept us from getting there. It's not a lack of education (or anything else) holding you back. You're breaking through the barriers.

In that same study of Harvard University Business School graduates, researchers found that, years after having gained the credentials and connections to succeed, three of those Harvard graduates were unemployed and *homeless.* Let me drive that point home: they graduated from Harvard Business School, and they were unable to get a job. They were living on the street. Let me ask you this: do you have somewhere to live? Do you have a job to go to? Then, technically, you're living better than a Harvard grad *today*.

God can use anyone—and in case you're wondering, that includes you. He sent some crazy girl like me to write this book for you, to encourage you to live out all God has called you to be. And I'll tell you what: I didn't go to Harvard Business School, either. But it ain't stopping me. I'm in the top 3% because I have written goals.

You are, too. The fact that you're actually writing them down just took you from somewhere in the masses to the top 3% of Americans. Congratulations. Finding that paper, finding that pen, taking time to listen, and taking action has just put you in some pretty good company.

You're in Good Company

Company like Will Smith. I was reading about someone who was invited to Will's home. The man walked into a big, gorgeous house with glass walls. But you couldn't see all the way through the walls, because the view was blocked with all these little pieces of paper. "What are those?" he asked Will.

There were notes and papers everywhere. Will smiled. "*That* is my new movie." It didn't look anything like a movie. It looked like a hot mess. "Let me walk you through it," said the visionary.

He explained how you have to have good characters, but you also have to have villains. You can't let people see the end from the beginning, so you have to have a plot twist. You have to make sure to have the ups and downs and emotional dynamics to make people feel, and a good storyline that will walk people through the plot.

His guest was blown away. It all seemed so confusing that he started rubbing his head. "Where do you start with something like that?"

Will smiled even wider.

"It's easy. You start at the end and then you write a plan to get there."

Will Smith starts each movie with an end in mind: *the goal.* What you're writing down today is your goal, your story—and that's going to reveal the beginning of your plan to get there.

"A goal properly set is halfway reached." —Zig Ziglar

Don't Mess with Me

When you know where you're going, people tend to get out of your way, even if they're not supposed to do so.

There was a big Night of Hope Event at a professional baseball stadium. David and I were on the field with Joel and Victoria

Osteen. The stadium was completely full. After the event, I started talking to people and got a little carried away. I looked up, and everybody else was gone. I saw some people that had walked us in earlier—they were heading toward an exit, off the field. I got myself in high gear and started heading that way. I didn't know where I was going—I was just trying to follow them. I thought they were going to the same place I was supposed to be.

The people made some twists and turns and walked past a couple of security guys, so I did, too. They were walking quickly, and darted through a door. I finally got to the same door. There was this guy standing in front of it, all big and puffed up. He had this earpiece in his ear and gave me a little sneer. I just looked at him like, "I've got to go," and brushed by him slightly, touching his arm as I passed through the small opening. The man didn't say a word to me.

I headed up some stairs, right around the corner. The people I was following were going through another door, so I hustled for that one too. There was yet another guard standing almost in front of the door, all official-looking, with all the right gear. I didn't want to get lost, so I reached past him to turn the door handle. I threw the door open and walked directly into Joel and Victoria's private dressing room! *Gulp.*

Thank goodness everyone was clothed.

They acted like it wasn't that big of a deal as I walked backward, stumbling over my words. Otherwise, I would've looked like a stalker! I thought, *Come on, people! Somebody do your job!* There had been three guys who were supposed to stop me from getting in there. I had no idea where I was actually going. I just knew I was going where those other people were going.

I guess I looked like, "Don't mess with me, I'm a woman on a mission." But I didn't even have a clue where I was headed. I was actually lost. If we're convinced we're on the right path and that we have a right to be there, people are going to get out of our way. People who are supposed to stop us won't. If we feel "less than," or we're wandering aimlessly, they'll never let us through. But we aren't wandering—we're writing our goals and heading straight for them.

Write this down: *Don't mess with me. I'm going somewhere good.*

God wants to take you somewhere better than good. He wants to take you all the way to *great*. He wants you to shrug off what the world told you that you couldn't do, and what the wrong people told you in order to slow you down. It's time to shrug off the mistakes you've made in your past, take off those scales from your eyes and start looking through the binoculars of faith.

You see, we can't see the future the way we're supposed to see it in the natural. We've got to see with eyes of faith. We've got to develop our imaginations to see bigger things than we can ask, think, or imagine. We've got to think with a God-sized imagination. After all, if we can do it by ourselves, our dreams are not big enough!

WHY DO I FEEL THIS WAY?

I know you're ready to start writing, but I want to prepare you for what you're about to feel.

You'll notice, as you start writing down your goals, that you're going to feel a little bit different. That's because writing goals is scientifically proven to elevate your heart rate. There's a motivation so primal that it's biological. Our blood pressure increases in a good way. Why? Because the spirit on the inside of you starts getting excited. The life that resides inside of you begins to spill out.

Don't look at your past to determine the possibilities of your future.

Don't look at your circumstances to decide the parameters of your present. Listen to the enthusiasm welling up inside of you.

J.C. Penney, who was a good Christian man, said, "If you give me a stock clerk with a goal, I'll show you a man that's going to make history. But if you give me a man that has no goal, well, I'll show you a stock clerk." I love that quote, because it proves that it doesn't matter where you start. It just matters *that* you start. It doesn't matter what happened to you. It doesn't matter what happened *because* of you. It doesn't matter what zip code you're in. It doesn't matter whether or not you've got your GED. It doesn't matter whether or not you were accepted to college. It doesn't matter whether or not people left you, betrayed you, or even passed over you for a promotion. I'm telling you right now: it does *not* matter where you start. You can't change your destination in a day, but you can change your direction. That's what we're going to do.

We're going to change our direction, today.

GET READY, SET, PRIME YOUR PUMP

I'm about to give you instructions that will take *three minutes* to execute, and that will help frame the best part of your life. Before I do, I need to help you prime your dream pump—to tap into your imagination like a little kid with a root beer keg in the backyard on their birthday.

I mean, I love watching little kids. They only think in the realm of *can* and *do*. Growing up to be Superman isn't out of the realm of possibilities to them.

I remember, back in the day, I wanted to be a Broadway star. The problem with that is Broadway wants all the girls to be about five feet tall. They need the women to be petite and cute to emphasize that the men are bigger and more masculine. There's nothing tiny about my five-foot-eleven-inch frame. The other thing is, they want you to be able to sing; but you know, whatever. I think it was more the height thing that held me back.

When I was a kid, we would get stuck at my great grandma's house for holidays. She had no toys, so we would head for the basement. When I say "Grandma's basement," how many of you can already smell a smell? Yeah. It was real, but it didn't slow me down. We had to do *something because we were bored*. This was my big chance to produce a just-off-Broadway show. I recruited my cousins and decided we would do *The Sound of Music*. I knew it was going to be awesome.

I assigned parts: "You're going to be the nun. You're going to be captain Von Trapp. You guys are going to be the kids, and we're going to sing. Great Grandma's basement is gonna be alive with the sound of music!"

We invited the parents downstairs and made them endure (I mean enjoy) all of the fruits of our 60- to 90-minute practice. We did this whole production number. In my head, it was fantastic—because my imagination was still intact.

You have to see it to be it. Today, if you put me in that same basement and told me to produce *The Sound of Music*, I would think it was cruel and unusual punishment. I'd just walk away. But it didn't stop me back then.

We're supposed to have childlike faith. We're supposed to see beyond the circumstances. That's the kind of thing God asks us to do. Genesis 11:6 says, "And now nothing will be restrained from them, which they have imagined to do." God says, "If you use your imagination—if you can see it, if you can put it out there, if you can put a vision to it—I can make it happen."

But we'll never leave where we are until we can see where we want to go.

And that's what a goal is!

A Goal is Like a Destination

If I called you and asked you to go on a road trip with me—if I told you that I'd be at your house in 15 minutes to pick you up—you would want to know where we're going, right? You would need to know how to pack. Are we going snow skiing? To the beach? To a conference?

What if we hit the road and didn't decide for an entire hour where we were going? What if we finally decided we wanted to lay on the beach, but had already spent an hour driving 80 mph toward Kansas? We'd have wasted our time and energy, and we have all the wrong stuff packed for the trip.

That's what happens when we don't have a goal, when we don't know where we're going. We waste a lot of time going the wrong direction and we're not prepared for what's coming up when we finally get there. We've got to know where we're going. No small plans are made here.

Let's go!

IT BEGINS

If the enormity of our dreams doesn't scare us just a little, then we may be walking by sight and not by faith. Our opportunity here is big… *way bigger* than we even think! It's about to get fast and furious. Do you have your pen and paper? Is your imagination station active and your dream pump primed? Okay. Let's write your goals.

Here are a few guidelines to help you reach your dreams:

Only Write 7-10 Goals

Why? In the past, I've had 10 spiritual goals, 10 financial goals, 10 personal goals and maybe 10 relational goals. For sure, 10 vacation goals. I've got 10 plans for my kids. I've got 10 plans for my dog, and I've got 10 plans for my plan. I've done stuff like that before. I ended up failing more than I achieved, and I walked away feeling defeated instead of accomplished.

Since then, I've read studies that made me realize that a lot of people end up feeling the same way! We divide our focus, miss the mark, and end up losing momentum instead of gaining it. There's an old adage that says, "If you chase too many rabbits, you won't catch any of them." Studies suggest that, if you write seven to ten goals, it allows you to narrow your focus so you can achieve what's in your heart.

This is why, if you're in the *Goal Getters Study Guide or Planner,* or using the tools from my website, there are only ten lines. You don't have to write down ten, but I want to challenge you to put down at least seven.

Write Your Goals Quickly

Set an alarm for *three* minutes.

Studies show that you should take no more than three minutes when writing your goals. Any longer than that, and you start talking yourself out of them. We start reasoning with ourselves: "Well, I could never do *that*…" Statements start popping into our heads such as, "That's really ambitious for someone like me," or, "I'm not really sure I can pull that off…"

No, no, no. Three minutes!

I want you to write your goals *right now,* while you're still reflecting on the two pivotal questions, *what would it take for this to be the most amazing year of my life? God, are You good with it?*

What's in your heart? Write it down. See how it feels. Be bold. No one is going to see it (for now) but you! What does it feel like to see it in black and white?

Is it challenging? A little scary? Do you feel peace in your heart, even though it's a stretch? Without faith, it's impossible to please God. I didn't ask if you're able to make this happen without God's help. I asked if, when you pass your brain and listen to your spirit, there's a peace down deep? The Bible says to be led forth with peace, so hold onto that one!

Or is your answer, "No, I feel kind of upset." Okay. God, we're going to pass on the upset and unrest in our spirit, and we're going to go with the goals about which we have peace.

Write it in the Present Tense

Let's recap so far:

- Only write 7-10 goals
- Write your goals quickly.
- And now, write your goals *in the present tense*.

2 Corinthians 5:7 says, "We walk by faith and not by sight." We're speaking faith words. We're thinking faith thoughts. It leads the heart out of defeat and into victory every time. We don't talk about it as if one day it could happen; we speak about it as if it's already happened.

Write things like they're complete. Write statements such as,

> "I weigh my perfect weight (whatever the number is). "
> "I live in a house that is paid off."
> "I'm accepted into (the school, the club, the job)."
> "I have received this promotion. I have the title of..."

Go ahead and write it as if it's in the present tense—and make sure you write it down, because you're going to need it.

Who Do You Think You Are?

When the going gets tough, we need to be able to reference our goals and say them as if they're already done. That helps our mind to settle it with finality. In Matthew 4, the devil came to Jesus with a specific purpose in mind: to tempt him. "Who do you think You are anyway, Jesus? Why do You think You've got this power?" If the devil was brash enough to poke Jesus, then yeah, the enemy's going to challenge you on your goals.

His line will be, "Who do you think you are anyway? Why do you think you have any right to this?" We need to answer the same way Jesus did in Matthew 4:4. Jesus' answer never changed, no matter how many times the enemy asked. He responded with the same three words every time.

He said, "*It is written.*"

Keep that goal in front of you, and you can tell the enemy, "This is my goal. It is written. I've talked with God about it, and He let me know that this is my direction. I know who I am. I know Whose I am. I'm a child of the Most High King, and I serve Jehovah Jireh, my Provider. He happens to be my Daddy. When you mess with the baby, all of heaven comes after you."

You've got to know who you are and Whose you are. You've got to write the vision and make it plain. Keep it in front of you. When the enemy comes to challenge it, you'll know what you're doing.

We can continue to do what we have been doing and continue to get what we have been getting... we can continue to be dissatisfied, looking around at the world and asking why they have it and we don't. *Or we can turn.* Tweak. Twist. Reach. Move. Think. Be intentional. It starts with writing your goals like you're getting ready to do.

Be Specific

Remember, clarity of vision brings clarity of life.

It worked for Oprah. She always knew that she would be a millionaire by 32. Not 35. Not 30. 32. Her ambition was, also, to be the richest black woman in America. The talk show host knew exactly where she was going, because she said these specific things: the age and the position. Nineteen years later, she was exactly where she said she would be, right on schedule. There's a difference between a resolution and a goal.

We were at a New Year's Eve party with some friends. A beautiful, young, up-and-coming couple was with us. I couldn't help but ask this medical school student and restaurant owner what their goals for the next year were. After all, they were *sharp*! They said things like, "Oh, I'm going to get more organized. I'm going to lose some weight. I want to have more time to myself." Their goals were loose and hard to quantify. There was really no way to tell if they were winning or losing.

They did what we all do: they spouted off the most common goals given by Americans when asked what they're working toward.

Most people answer, "I want to…

- save money.
- get out of debt.
- get closer to God.
- read more.
- organize the house.
- quit smoking.
- lose weight.
- spend more time with the family.

Do those answers sound like something you'd say?

Come on, be honest. We've all given them. It's nice table talk at a party… but not a solid goal. They're typically vague New Year's resolutions, but they're not attainable. That's why we haven't reached them and we tend to give up so quickly. We set ourselves up for failure. It's as loose as a guilty man's alibi—terribly vague, as broad as the day is long. They are almost impossible to measure. So how do you know if you've won?

I know you like to win. So we're framing your thinking for that. You're going to write your 7-10 specific goals. You're not going to just store them in your thoughts where they can get fuzzy or forgotten. You're writing them down because it adds clarity to your dream.

For example, maybe you want to work with animals. But what does that *mean*? Does that mean being a veterinarian? Being a veterinary assistant? Being a zookeeper? Leading a safari? Working at a dog shelter? *Opening* a dog shelter?

This is the time to clarify. Write quickly, within three minutes.

Does working with animals mean moving to Africa, going to veterinary school, or starting volunteer work at a local shelter? There's a big difference among these options. Nobody likes to shoot in the dark. Where exactly do you want to go? What do you want to be? What's your dream? Write it down. Make it plain.

The things I'm telling you aren't just ideas I invented out of thin air. It's God's idea. Habakkuk 2:2 says, "Then the Lord answered me and said: 'Write the vision and make it plain on tablets, that he may run who reads it.'" Write it down where you can see it, and be specific. I want you to say out loud right now, "I'm going to be specific." You need to hear yourself say that.

Is one of your goals financial? Are you thinking about financial increase? Do you want to have more money in the bank? Okay. How much is "more"? $5? $500? $5,000? Do you want to start a savings account so that you can work toward buying a house?

Are you going to start investing? Are you opening a credit account? Are you getting a jar and putting it in your closet to collect change and one-dollar bills? Let's get specific about what "financial increase" means to you. Then, you will know exactly when you hit your mark.

Maybe you want to lose weight (and we all said, "Amen," followed by, "Pass the pie, please!") How much weight? Do you want to lose 10 pounds this year? Is that the big win? Maybe it's only five pounds, and then you get to celebrate. Maybe it's 25. If we don't know where the finish line is, how will we know when we've won?

Write your specific goals down.

In sales, they teach you to be *crystal clear* in what you offer to people. The more precise you are, the better people will respond. There was a study that quantified these results. If we say something as vague as, "Can you spare any change?" We can expect a 44% rate of affirmative responses.

When we clarify it a little more, by asking, "Can you spare a quarter?" The affirmative response rate jumps to 64%! That's almost a 50% gain! When we get very specific, and say something like, "Can you spare 37 cents?" The study showed that 75% responded and followed through! Three-quarters of the people did what was asked of them!

This even works on ourselves. The clearer we are with ourselves and our future goals, the more we will respond to them!

> *"The trouble with not having a goal is that you can spend your life running up and down the field and never score."*
> —Bill Copeland

YOUR GOALS LIST

It's time! With pen in hand, tell Alexa to set a timer for *three* minutes. Write your specific goals in the present tense.

Dream big, baby! This is about to be your *best year yet*!

MY GOALS

1. _____

2. _____

3. _____

4. _____

5. _____

6. _____

7. _____

8. _____

9. _____

10. _____

"You're a #goalgetter!"

Step Two:

GET A VISION: TURN YOUR DREAMS INTO GOALS

TURN YOUR GOALS INTO VISION

I was a fan of Dr. Seuss when I was a kid. *Hop on Pop* and *One Fish, Two Fish, Red Fish, Blue Fish* were a couple of my favorites. I love this grown up quote that sounds rather "Seussy" to me, and is perfect for this moment:

> *"Your mind is a garden; your thoughts are the seeds.*
> *The harvest will bring either flowers or weeds."*

A single thought, much like a single raindrop, won't make a garden bloom. If you think about your goals once, and then walk away, you won't get the benefits of eating from the fruit. I'm actually watching a summer thunderstorm, right this minute. I saw the wall of rain heading for me. When it hit, I had to move inside from the front porch. Why? The presence of a single raindrop would never have moved me back into the house, but many raindrops together...that's power! The sheer force of their number moved me.

Writing your goals once and walking away is like a single raindrop. But many thoughts (compelling mental images with strong emotions resulting from writing your goals and reviewing them many times) create a powerful synergy of raindrops that saturate and nourish the ground from where your garden harvest grows. I know I'm getting kind of artsy with you. But what I really need you to do is pick up your hoe and start working. This garden ain't gonna plant itself. And truthfully, your momma don't work here. It's all you, baby!

The good news is that you were born for this. It's your dream. It's your burning desire. Now, you're taking these dreams-turned-goals to the next level. You're going to start walking toward living your dream. You're in the process of making the best investment of your life. *You.* Warren Buffet says, "When you invest in yourself, you get a 1,000% return." That's why I know it's safe to believe in you and what you're doing, even though we may have never met.

We're going to get the vision. We're going to make it plain so we can run with it. And we're going to make it fun in the meantime!

WHEN THE VISION IS CLEAR, RESULTS APPEAR

Clarity of vision brings clarity of life.

Are you seeing what you want to see out of life yet? Let's make sure we can see it to be it. If we haven't had clarity before, that may be why we haven't gotten results.

I was a tall kid in fourth grade, so my seat was always toward the back of the room. I couldn't see the board very well, and it gave me headaches. I got frustrated. My mom took me to the optometrist and I had to get prescription glasses. I'd like to tell you that I looked cute and smart. Instead, I looked kind of nerdy (but at least I could see the board). My headaches went away, and I could do my work again. My life got better in many areas, just because I could see more clearly. I knew what to do and how to do it.

Clarity is what we get when we turn our goals into a full-color, internalized vision.

Visualization

Have you ever used the power of visualization?

God did it first. He thought it, saw it in His mind's eye, said it and it happened. What happens in your life—any endeavor—begins first in your mind, through visualization.

Visualization is used by the most successful salespeople. Have you ever gone to a new car dealership and listened to a salesperson? They ask, "Can you see yourself driving this car?" Eventually you say, "Yes, I can certainly see myself driving this car." What's funny is that you may never have noticed that kind of car before. You thought, maybe it just came on the market. But once you drive it and notice it, suddenly, you see them everywhere!

One of the powers of visualization is that what's in the borders of the realm of possibility can be brought into reality. We stop simply seeing just within our mind, and we start seeing in our physical world. Then, the next thing you know, you're watching other people drive down the street in your dream, and you're trying to figure out how to make the payments! What a motivator!

Years ago, there was a man driving with his friend in Hawaii. They saw the home of the late Elvis Presley. The driver said to his friend, "Can you imagine living in a house like that?"

The other man replied, "No I sure can't!"

The first man, a successful man said, "And you never will, because you cannot be what you cannot see!"

Your subconscious mind has the ability to push your life in the direction of your dreams through the power of visualization. Become the person who can envision the future with great clarity! You have to see it to be it! What are you ready to see right now?

Tony Robbins says that setting goals is the first step to turning the invisible into the visible. Doesn't that sound a lot like 2 Corinthians 5:7? "We walk by faith and not by sight." God is the "OG" motivational guru ("Original Gangsta" for my friends over 40, and a huge compliment in millennial language). He's the One who set that up in the first place. Tony and the rest of the crew took their cues from the Creator. We're taking things out of the spirit realm, the unseen realm, and we're putting them into the physical realm of the Earth so that we can see them.

Don't Be a Statistic

One of our pastor friends who's on the board of our multi-state, multi-campus church came to town and spent a few days with us, working on our plans for the church's next year. I went to the front desk of the Hyatt to pay our friend's bill. I talked to a guy named Zach and got the bill for the room. After I looked it over I asked, "Zach, this bill looks really cheap. I think we got charged the wrong rate."

He said, "Oh no, we're not on our holiday, rate. We're on a 'We need more people here' rate."

"Are you kidding me?" I asked.

He replied, "Yeah, the first two weeks of January are always dead."

I was confused. After all, this is south Florida. "Really? Why?"

"Because everybody's doing their New Year's resolutions—they're meal prepping, they're going to the gym and they're saving money."

I was concerned for them. "Man, that must be really hard on the hotel."

He knew the drill. "Not really. By the third week of January, everybody gives up on the resolutions, and we make more money than ever. We'll be booked up."

Statistics say that 25% of people give up on their New Year's resolutions—those vague goals—within the first week of January. Sixty percent of the remaining people with poorly-formed resolutions will give up within the first six months. Here I am quoting Zach from the Hyatt, because that's the way it goes.

Don't let those statistics make you put this book down, call your friend and say, "I just knew it, Ed. We shouldn't have bought this book and started this journey." That's the *old us*. We made resolutions but then lost our focus. We lost what we couldn't see. Out of sight, out of mind.

The *old us* didn't have their 7-10 specific goals written in the present tense. The past us weren't about to internalize them, providing a clear vision. I'm going to show you how to keep what we want to happen in front of us so that we don't lose it or forget it.

> *"It must be borne in mind that the tragedy of life doesn't lie in not reaching your goal. The tragedy lies in having no goals to reach."*
> —Benjamin E. Mays

FOR THE NEXT 30 DAYS

Darren Hardy interviewed several of the most successful people in the world. Do you want to know the two things all of them have in common?

Number one: they're committed to personal growth. You've already shown that.

Number two: they're committed to writing down their goals. You might think, "I already did that." We did it *once*, but can you recite them? Probably not. *Yet.*

Our goals live outside of us, but not inside of us. Yet. We're moving and leaving the past behind. We're working on making "yet" a part of our vocabulary that we don't use anymore.

"By recording your dreams and goals on paper, you set in motion the process of becoming the person you most want to be. Put your future in good hands—your own."
—Mark Victor Hansen

I know you've started down a trail like this before. You might have even written your goals down, last time. But then, you got to the end of the year and reviewed them on December 30th (while trying to figure out what you were going to do on New Year's Eve). You started panicking: "Aw, snap. I messed up. I didn't reach my goals! What were they again? Eh, I'll do better next year."

That's not vision. That's what the 25% of people who gave up in the first week did. That's not focus. That's not internalizing your purpose. That's just scribbling on a napkin over a casual conversation. Let's increase that exponentially by putting some vision in front of it and some intention behind it.

Focus on Success

We've been looking for our future but not seeing it. *Mention brings focus.* So let's start talking about our goals in order to dial in on that focus for our preferred future. We're going to do this for 30 days.

Here's the step that will take you from the typical "I have goals on a piece of paper somewhere" to "I wrote it, I did it, and I put the trophy on the shelf." You're going to focus and internalize your 7-10 goals until they become a part of you. We'll make them easy to focus on. We're going to walk through an exercise to get them to stick.

It's time to flex your hustle muscle. God isn't going to simply drop success into your lap. He's going to give you a plan. He's going to give you a purpose. He's going to give you a pursuit, and then He's going to ask you to pursue it. I'm going to tell you how. Are you ready?

How do you move toward your goals?

- You're going to *write your goals down.*
- Every day for 30 days.
- You're going to write them down in a very specific way.

Before I share more about the *what*, I want you to understand the *why*

REPROGRAMMING YOUR BRAIN FOR SUCCESS

You're preparing to capitalize on the premise of neuroplasticity: the reprogramming your brain for success. I do an entire study on understanding how the mind works in my *T12 Transformation Program* on my website *NicoleCrank.com.* Goals are one part of it; but we also dive into transformation related to every major part of your life.

Utilizing neuroplasticity allows us to pull up the roots of "I can't" and lay down the roots of "I can." This is a mental workout that's training your brain to reign. You are literally programming the computer of your mind to reach your goals on autopilot!

Life Before GPS

> *"All successful people have a goal. No one can*
> *get anywhere unless he knows where he wants*
> *to go and what he wants to be or do."*
> —Norman Vincent Peale

Reprogramming your brain involves plugging in specific coordinates, like a GPS. I love GPS. I might be able to find my way around without it, but it's just so easy to use. I don't have to think. It just tells me where to go and how to get there. It's the closest thing to autopilot, outside of Tesla.

We were on a road trip from Florida to St. Louis when David got tired of driving our motorhome. Let me just add that driving this vehicle is not my thing. The RV is big and cumbersome. I was happy to navigate the paper maps while he drove—that's my gift! But when he needed a break, he closed his eyes and took a nap.

I'd been looking at the map and I was pretty sure I remembered how to get home: Take Highway 60 toward Highway 285, right?

Bypass Atlanta and the traffic. Easy peasy. I headed that way for about 90 minutes while David slept.

He woke up and started to panic. I was so confused. *What's his deal? We're okay. I had no accidents.* We had gas. In fact, I was pretty proud of myself! Then, I realized the problem: I'd driven us all the way to Atlanta—an hour out of our way. Now, we'd need *another* hour just to get back on track. Our 12-hour trip would take two *more* hours! Great…

That's the way we often are on our way to our goals. We write them once because it's New Year's Eve, or we're in a class, or we're reading a book like this one, or someone tells us we have to do it. Then, we don't even look at them anymore. We think we know where to go. We're all proud of ourselves. Before we know it, we look up at the calendar and it's six months later. We're not where we thought we'd be at all. *What happened?* We think. *I wrote my goals!*

Am I Talking to You Right Now?

Let's fix this so we'll never live out that scenario again. We're going to use the premises of neuroplasticity to program your brain for success. We're going to write down your 7 to 10 goals:

   ✓ *With pen and paper*

Why use pen and paper? It physically engages you in the process. I'll make it easy for you: you can get out your *Goal Getters*

Study Guide, or go to my website *NicoleCrank.com* to download a free tool I have for you. (It's 30 days of downloadable pages that include quotes and Scriptures!)

You're going to write your goals, with pen and paper:

✓ *Every day for 30 days*

Every day.

I'm going to say it again. Every day for 30 days.

This is programming your brain. Each time you think a thought, you create or reinforce a neuron connection in your brain. Every time that those neurons are "fed" by a thought, we "grow" the neuron. Tentacles, that look like roots, form in the brain.

We're literally rooting and grounding our goals into our brains. We're moving our goals from the intellectual realm into the physical world. The "roots" in our brain, which are grown by our daily thoughts and writing our goals, are powerful enough to physically shift the folds in our brain.

You're changing the way you think, and it's going to change the way you live.

To do this, you can use your own notebook, you can use your own journal, or you can use the things that I've provided for you because they make it fun, recordable and functional.

You're going to write down your 7-10 goals every day with pen and paper for 30 days, *and*:

    ✓ *Don't look back at what you've written before.*

Yeah. Can't look back at the past. No looking. No peeking.

Write your 7-10 goals every day for 30 days, without looking back at what you've written before. A fresh piece of paper. A fresh list. Work that training for reigning into your brain-ing. It's okay if you forget one. It's okay if you forget the wording. The point isn't perfection—it's recall. Don't look back! Work your brain. We're drilling it into your psyche. Every day, just do your best to remember.

This takes your goals from a whim to a purpose—from accidental to intentional—from something you thought about once upon a time to something you're living! Twenty-five percent of people abandoned their New Year's Eve goals within the first week. Sixty percent of remaining resolution-setters abandoned them within six months.

So why are we doing this exercise?

Because it will keep you from becoming one of them. Most of the people don't write it down. You're halfway there by just doing that! Only 3% of people write down their goals. You're already in the top echelon. Now, if you do this little exercise, you're going to get your vision in front of you.

Write your 7-10 goals with pen and paper, every day for 30 days, not looking back at what you've written before…

> ✓ *Every morning BEFORE work (or you will cop out)*

"Why before work?" you ask. "I need my coffee," you complain. I understand that you need your coffee, but here's why: you get to work. "I'll do it before dinner," you promise yourself. Then you get busy; you have a bad day; you go home and scrounge up something to eat. You've got 14 things you have to do. Something inevitably comes up and eats some of your time. You do eight of the things, and now you're tired. You go to bed and wake up the next morning, one day behind in the race to reach your dreams. You didn't do it yesterday, and the enemy's going to try the same tricks today. He's already stealing your future with distractions.

So set that alarm. Get your java. Keep your *Goal Getters Study Guide and Planner* next to the coffeemaker. Be ready to chase your dreams first thing in the morning!

Time for a Pop Quiz

Let's do this for the first time right now! Accuracy doesn't matter. Write down your goals again, to the best of your recollection. Start programming your brain. Reach in there and see what you can pull out. It might be more than you think.

GOALS

1. _____

2. _____

3. _____

4. _____

5. _____

6. _____

7. _____

8. _____

9. _____

10. _____

POST-IT NOTE VISIONS

Now, let's take some action steps to get this thing going.

I want you to see it so much that you're able to be it. I want you to start by organizing what you see. Begin with one area of organization, and it will grow. Organize what you have in your mind.

Even if my house is a mess, my closet is still organized. Here's why I do that. I usually get dressed in my closet. I go in there and pick out my clothes. If my closet is a mess, I feel like my life is a mess. But when I'm getting ready in the morning—even if the coffee in the pot is three days old, even if the bed's not made, even if it looks like my house is a wreck and has been ransacked like I've been robbed—if I can get into my closet, a small, controlled area that's organized, I can begin organizing my thoughts for the day, and thus, organizing my life.

That's what I'm trying to help you do. Write one goal on each Post-it Note.

Now, stick the notes in places around your house that you're going to see every day. Put one above the toilet paper roll—you know you're going there (like, you're literally *going* there). Put one in the refrigerator—you know you're going there. Put one on your phone. You know you look at that 97 times a day. Put one next to the TV remote. You know you're going to reach for that a few times a day. Put one on the speedometer in your car. You know your eyes will be there. Put one on your computer screen at work, because you gotta go there. Put them in places where you're going to see the vision before you.

Believe the Vision

There was a sixth-grade boy named Stevie. He was born in the wrong zip code. Even worse, he stuttered. His teacher gave him an assignment. She said, "I want you to write a paper on who you want to be when you grow up."

Stevie had seen a man being funny on television, and he thought, *Wow, wouldn't that be a great job—to make people laugh? I want to do that.* So he wrote his paper about being a comedian. When his teacher read his paper, she called him to the front of the class. As he hustled up there, he thought, *Oh, she must really like my paper!*

She said, "Stevie, I want to ask you a question. Does anybody in your family—anybody in this classroom, even—know someone who's ever been on television?"

Stevie said, "No... no ma'am."

She said, "I want you to rewrite your paper with something that's *real*."

Boy, can you believe that?

Stevie went home and told his dad, "I've got to rewrite my paper. I messed up, Dad."

His father said, "Let me see what you wrote." Then he said, "Stevie, you can rewrite that paper for your teacher, but I want you to take this and put it on your bathroom mirror. I want you to read it every morning before you go to school, and every night before you go to bed."

That's exactly what Steve Harvey did every day. We can't let the world tell us who we are or what we're going to be. We have to believe the vision that God has placed in our hearts.

Your Past Doesn't Determine Your Future

I was privileged to meet one of the students at our church through Twitter. This particular teen was extremely bright, hard working, and he attended one of the best schools in our city. From the savvy that this high school student had, you might think he was a blue blood, bred with a silver spoon in his mouth.

Actually, the opposite was true. He was born with challenges that could've easily kept him from reaching for the stars. He could have thought, "I'm not from the right zip code." His parents were only 16 when he was born and split up when he was very young. Life didn't make it easy for him to achieve his dreams. He could have easily been just another statistic.

However, he had a great mentor who set him onto a path for success. At 14 years old, he started his own marketing and consulting business. He's worked with companies like Ford, AT&T, Verizon and K-SWISS. Wouldn't you know it, this high school kid was even managing Steve Harvey's social media account!

Now, you might be thinking, "Man, it's a shame that Steve Harvey can't afford anyone but a high school kid to be his social media guy. I mean, really?" Oh no, no, no. You see, this student had some circumstances, but he didn't get stuck where he started. Steve Harvey is just *one* of his many clients.

He started believing what God had to say about him, and it breathed new life into him. Now, at the ripe old age of 22, he's already had speaking gigs at the White House, Stanford, Harvard, MIT, Megafest and Disney World. He's been recognized among the top 100 Most Influential African Americans, according to *Ebony Magazine.*

Today, the company he founded is one of the fastest-growing minority-owned businesses in St. Louis.

He never let his past determine his future!

His story reminds me of a college girl. She came home for Christmas break and saw some goals on the refrigerator that her dad had written: "Love my wife more. Have a date night. Be more productive at work. Lose some weight."

She thought, *If he's got goals, I'll just add to Daddy's list, "Pay my daughter's rent."* Then, the man's son saw it and decided to get in on this, too. He added, "Make my son's car payments." When dad went back to the refrigerator for some leftovers, he saw the refrigerator door. He thought, "What are my kids adding on here?" He added his own new goal:

"Wean my kids off of financial aid."

Suck it up!

You've got to have goals, and you've got to keep them straight. But you've got to have them in front of you so that you know exactly what they are. That's what it says in Proverbs 29:18: "Where there is no vision"—when you can't see what God has for you; when your vision has been clouded by doubt and circumstances; when you're not using your eyes of faith; when you're not writing down your goals—"the people perish."

What does "perish mean?" Buy some celery at the grocery store, put it in the vegetable drawer and leave it there for a year. When you come back, you'll see what "perish" looks like. It stinks. It's wilted. It's nasty and it's almost dead. If that's what your life looks like right now, if that's what your future is shaping up to be, here I am with the water (sustenance to revive you) that you need. If you take semi-wilted celery and put it in cold water and leave it there, it will start sucking that up. It will start to come back to life!

That's what the washing of the water of the Word does for you: it brings life back into you. God doesn't want you to lead a perishing life. God gives us a plan for how to reach our goals. It's time to suck it up (just like celery) and start dreaming again!

You aren't called to perish! You're called to make the vision plain upon Post-its so that he who reads it may run!

Now buy those Post-it Notes!

Keep Your Attention on Your Intentions

Just like Steve Harvey, we're supposed to put our goals somewhere we can see them. On our bathroom mirror. In our car. Somewhere we can see it every day. That's why I developed and use the *Goal Getter* paper Planner that tells me where to be and when to be there. (I tried using my Google Calendar, but sometimes Siri lies.)

On every page, I put my top five goals for the day. John 10:10 warns us, "The thief comes to steal, to kill and destroy." He's here intentionally working toward his goal to steal, kill and destroy your future—to steal, kill and destroy your dream.

The way that happens is this: you set your alarm 20 minutes early and think, "Okay, tomorrow's going to be a good day. I'm going for this thing!" Then you wake up, and the dog has pottied on the carpet. One of the kids broke a glass on the kitchen floor. You get to your car and you're low on gas. You've got to stop at the gas station, and now you're late for work (and one of your goals was to be on time).

The enemy's going to try and kill our goals. We have to keep ourselves focused. When you keep your attention on your intentions, it makes you successful. But you have to be intentional about it.

On day 31, after you've been looking at your Post-it Notes, you're going to start adding images to your goals. We level up again!

You're going to take the vision and you're going to make it plain!

GET OUT YOUR VISION BOARD: NOW, ADD IMAGES

The *Cambridge Dictionary* says that the old saying, "Seeing is believing," means that, if you see something yourself, you will believe it to exist or be true, despite the fact that it is extremely unusual or unexpected.[2]

I have mentioned 2 Corinthians 5:7—it says, "Walk by faith, not by sight." Why? We have such a limited human perspective that what we see tends to be true. We easily believe it. But what we can't see—the invisible hand of God, His plans, how it all

---

2. *Cambridge Dictionary.* "Unexpected," Accessed 2020. *https://dictionary.cambridge.org/us/dictionary/english/unexpected*

comes together, the master plan—is so much bigger than we can see with our eyeballs.

We need to cut a faith keyhole from our realm of what is into the realm where God is—from our existing life to the realm of what could be. We need to change how we see. Or, we could say, we need to change our *vision*.

Excited by the Vision

For a while in my life, I wore contact lenses. They were such a hassle. Sometimes, they hurt. I had to carry around a bunch of gear. I could only wear disposable lenses, so they were expensive.

In an attempt to make them fun, I got green lenses. I loved them! When I looked at myself, I could see something new and different. (Honestly, I think I look much better with green eyes, and I plan on talking to God when I get to heaven about why in the world my eyes are brown!) Isn't it funny. I liked my contacts more for how they made me look than for how they helped me see.

Of course, the biggest reason I wore them was so that I could see better. I'd had glasses since the fourth grade for seeing distance, especially in the classroom. They improved my vision, but that didn't really excite me. It should have. Instead, a cute little cosmetic change tickled my fancy.

I think that's how a lot of us operate today. The process of tapping into and correcting the vision for our lives doesn't always excite us. The new house does. A new car does. A new relationship does. A cosmetic change does. These things make us giddy. But they aren't the long-term goal or the key to lasting happiness.

What is it that we need to change our vision? What we see. How we see it—no matter how far or close we are to it. That's one of the benefits of having a vision board. It isn't expensive. In fact, it can be a lot of fun to design. The end product can be really cute, cool, have swag (whatever your word is). It's like adding a corrective lens to our future. We stop seeing our dreams all fuzzy in the distance, and we begin to pull in our designed, purposed, intended, and prayed-for future with 20/20 clarity.

The coolest thing about my contact lenses is that I don't even need them anymore. (No, I didn't get Lasik. God just did something creative!)

Corrective Lenses

My husband and I were living out in the country, and I was running out of disposable lenses. I'd actually developed a condition called GPC (Giant Papillary Conjunctivitis). My eye enzymes reacted to the contact lenses with irritation—I would get a rash underneath my own eyelid. *Ouch.* I didn't want to wear glasses, but I'd put up with the pain until now. It was just getting worse.

Before I finish the story, I want to point out that so many of us are here right now. We've set goals before. We've tried to dream. Maybe we've even created a vision board. But we stopped looking at it because some things didn't happen. Life got tough. We aren't even sure why, right now. All we know is that things got too uncomfortable to keep pursuing our vision. We were allergic to our own life enzymes, and it was causing us to be uncomfortable.

I prayed and asked God to please heal my eyes so that my contacts wouldn't hurt so much.

But God...

Since we lived on a horse farm in a rural area (back around the year 2000, before we were senior pastors), the closest vision center was at Walmart. I made an appointment and went in to see the optometrist. He examined my eyes and then pulled back and made a face at me that made me feel like I was five years old and I'd gotten caught stealing a cookie.

"Who told you that you need contacts?"

...he asked, with layers of sarcasm so thick I needed a shovel to get through them.

"Um, every optometrist since I was in 4th grade," I answered. His snooty-looking expression changed to a puzzled one. "Why?" I wanted to know.

He said, "Because you have 20/20 vision."

Are you kidding me? Nope. I'm not kidding you at all.

We serve a God who is exceedingly, abundantly above all we can ask, think or imagine. My limited "faith vision" only asked God to heal the GPC on my eyes. Instead, He healed my eyes all together! Here I am, 20 years later, no glasses. No contacts. No Lasik.

What does this have to do with your vision board? You need a vision board to correct your vision every single day so you can see clearly what God has planted in you, instead of what you *think* you can accomplish on your own. It does no good if you make one and then put it in the closet.

Make your vision board.

Make one for home and one for work. Take a picture of it and make it the screensaver on your phone. *See yourself* in these places through the corrective lens of faith on your vision board. Then, one day, you'll believe it so deeply that you can take the lens off and see your future just as clearly without it. But this won't happen until you can *see yourself* succeeding. Say that out loud, right now. (Saying is such a big part of getting what you see.) Say, "I can see myself there." Now, say out loud where you see yourself...come on! Do you want it or not?

You need to see the vision so much that it starts to become normal in your brain. You need to see it so often that, when Oprah *does* call, you won't stutter once. You'll know exactly what to say. After all, you've seen this situation at least 100 times before in your mind. God is going to restore your vision. I'm in our office in St. Louis one week, then in West Palm Beach the next week. How many vision boards do you think I have? I've got two, because I can't go a whole week without looking at my vision board. I've got to keep it before me. I've got to make it plain.

YOU HAVE TO SEE IT TO BE IT

When the vision is clear—when you can see it—you don't have to look at it to know what it is. When you know exactly what your vision is, results just seem to happen. Write this down in the margin of this book and read it out loud ten times:

"When the vision is clear, results appear."

In Genesis 30, Jacob and his uncle Laban were in the livestock business together. Jacob was really getting ripped off. He was doing all the work while his uncle (the boss) was getting rich. (That might be where you are right now.) But Jacob had a vision for his future. He made a deal with Laban: his uncle would keep all the pristine, perfect animals (the ones everyone wanted). In exchange for his labor, Jacob could keep the few leftover, spotted animals (the ones nobody else wanted). It didn't seem like a very good deal for Jacob!

But Jacob had vision, a goal, a creative idea, a plan. It might seem crazy to someone who wasn't focused on a preferred future, but he felt that God led him to do something which took a lot of faith and follow-through. He would hold branches with leaves over the animals while the sun shone through. The sun cast spots of sunlight and shadow on them. When he looked at a white sheep, it looked like a spotted sheep. You see, you've got to see it to be it. You've got to make the vision clear.

Wouldn't you know it, Jacob's idea worked!

Whenever a new baby animal was born, they had spots! Jacob cleaned up! Jacob's vision was so clear. Not only could he see it, but the other animals could, too! That's why you need a vision board. You need to see your goals every day!

For the last few days, you've been writing down your 7-10 goals every day without looking back. Now, the vision is taking shape in your mind and becoming rooted there. Your vision is becoming a part of you. Now, we're really going to take that vision to the next level. We're going to take it outside of you, to reflect it back *inside*. Now, we get out the magazines. We do some Photoshop, or some cut-and-paste. We go searching for fun pictures on the internet. We are going to make our vision "real" and spot our goats!

My Vision Board

Let me tell you about one of my vision boards.

I'm going to share some of my vision with you. You may think I'm *crazy*, but just watch how things work. A few years ago, I'd never preached in a secular arena before. On my vision board, I cut and pasted a picture of a big arena. I found a picture of me and Photoshopped it standing on the stage, speaking to all the people. It was a totally doctored photo, but I could clearly see me doing it as if it had already happened.

Sure enough, in the beginning of the very next year, I spoke to 7,000 women at a conference in a secular arena. I saw that photo hanging in my office every day for a year. The vision was clear. My faith was built, and look at what God has done.

He gave me what I was believing for.

There was another picture I put on my vision board recently. It was a photo of my book, *Hi God, It's Me Again.* I was believing that the Spanish version, *Hola Dios*, would be able to get into some of the hard-to-reach areas of the Spanish population, and that it would touch their lives.

Sure enough, the doors to communist Cuba opened up to us.

Out of nowhere, I met the President of the Cuban Council of Churches, and God gave me favor with him. They arranged a conference with 1,500 Cuban pastors. *Hola Dios* was distributed to all of their churches. A year earlier, I had put the picture on my vision board. Look what God made happen. It isn't a coincidence.

I had more pictures of vision projects that came through, too. But I have to tell you about one of my favorite ones. I had a picture of me and Oprah sitting down together onstage. It looked super real. Except it's fake. Again, I was totally Photoshopped in there. But you know what? I believe—Oprah, if you're reading this, hello!—I believe, one day, Oprah and I are going to be sitting together, rapping about overcoming your past, setting goals and living the life of your dreams,

(Hey O… call me!).

What God wants to do in your life, you can get the literal vision for on your vision board. I believe that God is going to bring it to pass.

Stretch Your Vision!

Whenever I sit down to a meal, in my head, I think I'm going to eat like a dainty girl. Then, I find myself eating everything on my plate and going back for seconds. More often than not, I am the last one at the table eating (and not because I am a slow eater). In polite terms, we can say that I expanded my original goal.

Expanding is the process of setting goals—places we want to go. You know, if we look at a map, the first thing we need to find out is where we are. The second thing we look for is where we want to go. As we work on expanding our vision by setting our goals, let's take the limits off for the moment. We will deal with those later. For now, let's dream!

God is very interested in stretching us. He wants to enlarge us.

> *Enlarge the place of your tent, and let the curtains*
> *of your habitations be stretched out; spare not;*
> *lengthen your cords and strengthen your stakes.*
> —Isaiah 54:2 (AMP)

God is basically saying, "Baby, this thing is going to be big! It's going to get tight and it's going to streeeeetch" (kind of like my pants on Thanksgiving Day!). God is a God of faith, and faith begins where the will of God is known. In order to even start thinking faith thoughts, we have to start setting goals. We have to start dreaming.

In order to know what faith words to speak, we have to have an idea of what our goal is. In order to start taking faith actions (the actions that move us toward things that don't exist yet), we have to think faith thoughts and speak faith words. *We have to have those goals.* This is the process of expanding.

Do you remember the toy Stretch Armstrong? He's kind of rough-looking and rubbery, and you could stretch him. I got one of those when I was five years old, and I would try and play with it by myself because my brothers and sisters weren't born yet. I could only stretch him so far. But when a friend would come over to the house, I would get on one side and they would get on the other and we would pull on Stretch Armstrong. It would get so big, I'd be like, "We're good. We'd better stop. It's too much! It can't expand anymore!"

But Stretch Armstrong never tore. *That's* the importance of staying the course all the way through this book. You are on one side of Stretch Armstrong, and I am on the other side; together, we're going to stretch your dream so far out. If you need more stretching, go to my website and get the *Goal Getters Study Guide* and the *Goal Getters Planner* (I am a planner *nut*, I take mine *everywhere*). I even designed a video course for those who are serious about actually living their dreams *this year!*

Life is going from "snack pack" size to God's size. In Jesus' name, we need a big vision. Stretch Armstrong and my Thanksgiving pants can handle it!

DON'T GET "BORED" WITH YOUR VISION —MAKE YOUR VISION BOARD FUN!

*The only thing worse than being blind
is having sight, but no vision.*
—Helen Keller

Have a strong vision. There's a lot to believe for in your life. It's time that your eyes see the details in full color. It's time to find pictures to support what you want to do.

- What will you do when you pay off your student loan? Snip it and put it on your vision board.
- What does your dream vacation look like? Find it on the internet and paste in on your board.
- How will you look at your perfect weight? Put your head on that body, and onto the vision board it goes.
- What kind of house will you buy when you save up that downpayment? You know what to do—let's get it done!

Close your eyes (mentally—you have to have them open to read this). I want you to think of a goal you have… whether it's a place you want to go, revenue numbers you want to hit, purchases or acquisitions you want to make, the job you want to have, graduating from school, or holding that baby in your arms. Now, I want you to see that picture in your head.

You can't head for a goal you can't see.

You need to be able to see with the eyes of your imagination, your heart, your faith. Let God illuminate that thing on the inside of you. Now, add that to your vision board.

In the next chapter, we're going to take these images and make a concrete action plan that will take us toward realizing our goals. Are you ready? Get your vision board set up, and let's move on to Step Three.

Step Three:

GET GOING: THE ACTION PLAN TO GET YOU THERE

LIGHTS, CAMERA, ACTION!

> *"Goals. There's no telling what you can do when you get inspired by them. There's no telling what you can do when you believe in them. And there's no telling what will happen when you act upon them."*
> —Jim Rohn

Let's get this party started. *Lights, camera, action!* You know what? If we have the lights and they're on, if we've got the cameras and they're rolling, but we don't have any action… There's nothing to record. *Action.* It's where the rubber meets the road. It's where most people fall off the train.

Maybe you dream. Maybe you talk about what you want to do. Maybe you even wrote down your goals on paper. Writing down your goals gives you a 42% likelihood of achieving them. You're almost halfway there. What's the difference between you and everybody else? You're going to act on them. That's what we're going to talk about in this next section of Goal Getters. Mark Twain said, "The secret of getting ahead is getting started." So, let's get to it!

THE MAP TO GET YOU THERE

Here is where we draw the MAP for reaching your goals! The way to achieve your goal is hustle—by drawing this map.

Let's talk about MAP. M.A.P. means to:

Measure
Assess
Plan

We're going to measure what's happening in our lives right now. We'll look at what we have measured, ask questions and assess options on how to get there, so that we can build a crystal-clear plan to take us there. Then, we have to do the deed.

If we don't have a destination in mind, we won't know how to plot the course, and we'll never know when we get there. The good news is that you can get anywhere in the world from right "here." You can get to Miami, New York City or even Venice, Italy. You can get to the place of your dreams as a business owner, kingdom-builder, artist, missionary, creative, author, healthy person, director, inventor—whatever, wherever, who-ever God has called you to be!

WHAT YOU MEASURE CAN BECOME A TREASURE

We can talk about plans, but we have to *do* the work if we want to see results. I'm proud of you for making it this far, but I can't leave you here. We are going all the way to your dream desti-nation together.

> *"But the noble make noble plans, and*
> *by noble **deeds** they stand."*
> —Isaiah 32:8

The "M" in MAP is for Measure.

You have to know where you are so that you can mark your progress. You have to be able to win and know when you do!

There are a lot of things we can and should measure in life—our health, wealth, emotional and mental well-being, and dreams. I can't tell you what you "should" measure; I can only stir your thoughts and get you thinking outside of the box.

Here are some things you could start with:

- Weight
- Percentage of body fat
- What you owe on your home
- Savings to buy a home
- Amount of money in investments/savings
- Monthly expenses
- What you owe on your credit cards
- The number of books you read last year
- The number of hours you spent in self-investment last year
- The daily amount of time spent seeking God/praying/ reading Scripture
- The number of days you journaled in a prayer/ life journal
- The number of hours per week you spent investing in family relationships
- The number of hours per week you spent investing in friend relationships

It's time for an examination!

In 2003, when I found out I was pregnant with my daughter, Ashtyn, I thought, *Okay, how big am I, really? Because in my head, I think I'm a size two, but I haven't been that small since first grade. So that can't be true!* I needed a real picture of my size (a realistic goal to work back to after she was born) so I wouldn't get depressed. *Without knowing where we're starting from, it's impossible to measure any progress at all.*

I measured my thighs, my waist, and my hips. And no, I am *not* sharing what those measurements were in my pregnancy or what they are today! I'm glad I did that, though, because it took me a year just to get back into my jeans (not even the shape I was before… just getting them zipped!) I'm just being real! We have to know where we started in order to know when we've made progress… yes, even when we don't like where we are today.

When we first started pastoring the church, my husband didn't want to know how many people were in the auditorium for Sunday services. It bummed him out. His dream was bigger than our reality. So his answer was to stay in the dark. I'd tell him, "Sweetie, we had 200 people today." But if I reported the next week, "We had 180 people," He would freak out!

"Twenty people didn't come? Why? Nicole, quit telling me about how many people we have." I kept counting and examining. (I just didn't tell him.)

Examining, or measuring, is basically synonymous with a corporate term called "benchmarking." It's tracking where you are by taking measurements and recording for historical comparison. If you don't know where you are, how do you know where to go from here? That's the question to ask.

We usually don't get so excited about benchmarking. But it's what led to the conversation I had to have with my husband not long after I reported 180 people on a Sunday morning. "Sweetie, did you know that our attendance has grown by 30 percent in the last three weeks?"

"What?" He liked the good news. In order to get to the good news (in order to know how much we had grown), we had to measure *all* the news—even when it wasn't what we wanted it to be. When numbers go down, that can teach us even more valuable things than when numbers go up!

> *"Do not despise these small beginnings, for*
> *the LORD rejoices to see the work begin."*
> —Zechariah 4:10

Don't be scared to look at where you are today. We have to examine and measure where we are so we know where we're starting. That's how we'll know how to get where we're going.

Today is the day. Measure now! Not tonight when you get home… right now! You can't just talk about it. I'm not letting you off the hook because you can talk the talk. You've got to walk the walk. Here's how we're going to walk it. You have to know, when you're walking, if you're winning.

Let's measure every single one of our goals, today.

AND THE 'A' STANDS FOR...

The "A" in MAP stands for Assess.

We need to assess where we are today so that we can develop an *action* plan by *asking*. Ask, "*How* are we going to do that?" If you're going to write a book, you have to start writing something—anything!

When? When are you going to start writing?

Where? Do you have a certain place where you want to write?

How? How will you write? Will you use a special notebook? A computer? An app?

What? What are you going to write? It doesn't have to be big.

No one else has to see it. There are options.

You can start a blog, journal every day, or research and write a first draft of a book proposal. It all starts with assessing and asking the right questions that will lead you to an action plan.

Where Focus Goes, Energy Flows

Asking questions will start energy flowing in the direction of your dreams.

I had a friend who told me he wanted to do $1 million in business a year. It was a specific goal. He knew the amount and the deadline. But it never went past that. I wanted to get his "almost a goal" out of his head and into reality. I wanted to ask some questions: "That's great. Let's make a MAP for that. How much business do you have to do per month?"

He didn't know. So, we figured it out: $83,333 a month. He was wowed, and a little nervous, at that number! I thought it was more attainable than he did, so I asked, "How much revenue do you have to bring in a week?" The answer was $19,230. He was still a bit intimidated. "Okay! Let's keep breaking it down. Divide that weekly number by five business days." It was $3,800 and some change per business day. A light started to come on in his eyes, and a smile started creeping across his face. He started to commit. "Hey, I can do that."

"Great," I said. "We're starting to develop our MAP—our daily, our weekly, our monthly, and our yearly goal." You see, you have to have them all. If you miss a day, you can't get discouraged. You've simply got to fold that into the week. Whether you're measuring calories, revenue, number of sales calls, or hours spent reading and educating yourself... where did you end up for the week?

Not on track with your goal? Don't get dismayed. Let's fold that into the month. "But I had a month that wasn't great," you respond. Fold that into the year. You need to know where you're going and how far away you are. Is the gap small? (I'm pinching two fingers together with about one inch in between.) Then we just need to do a little more. Is the gap large? (I'm spreading my arms open wide.) That requires more asking, and a new plan.

Do we need to go out and do some Facebook ad marketing? Do we need to touch all clients and see if they've got any new business? Do we need to send out emails? Do we need to send out direct mail? What are we going to do? You might be thinking, "Well, I don't have a business that's going to do $1 million. I don't have a business at all yet."

All right—let's talk about you.

Let's Figure Out Where We Are

What are your goals? Maybe your goal is to pay off a credit card. How much do you owe? $12,843? Okay. At least you know where you're starting from, right? That's measurement. Okay.

How much do you need to pay that off? Let's say you need $1,150 a month. Great. How much is that per paycheck? $575—great. Can you do that? Maybe that's kind of tight. All right. What else are we going to do? Google it. Did you know that eBay says the average American has 50 unused items in their household that will bring an average of $3,000? There are other ways. There are other plans. There are garage sales, there's always something we can do.

Maybe your goal is to save to buy a house. How much do you have to have in savings? $10,000? $20,000? We need to know where you're at today. How much more do you have to make? $1,500? $3,500?

Maybe you want to lose weight. I know this is going to be unpopular... take a deep breath and step on the scale. You can't celebrate losing a pound if you don't know that you lost it.

Maybe you want a career. Maybe you want to get into college. Where are you today? What career do you want? What credits do you need? Let's go ahead and start writing it down. We're going to measure where we are today so we can do the second thing in our Goal Getters MAP Action Plan: assess. Let's assess what's happening.

Now that we have a measurement, let's figure out exactly what to do.

Say we have $1,000 in the bank and we know we want to save up $10,000 to buy a house. We want to assess where we are so we can put together an action plan. We already have $1,000 in the bank, so we need $9,000 more. Say we want to do that in a year. That's $750 per month that we need to save. If we get paid twice a month, we need to set aside $375 per paycheck. Now, we can really assess what we're doing. We have a solid action plan for every single paycheck that we can use for the house savings.

Ask Yourself Some Questions

Here are some question ideas to prime the pump—however, *you* are the one who knows the tough questions in your own life. You know exactly where you want to grow and improve. So measure every metric and every item that has to do with your goal.

(Here's a shameless plug for some recommended reading: *Solving Your Money Problems* by David Crank!)

Financial Questions

- Do I have a budget?
- Am I sticking to my budget?
- What weeks do I stay on budget?
- How much do I go over/under budget each week?

Then, let's get even deeper…

- How much should I spend each week?
- How much did I go over/under in my spending each week?
- How much did I save or invest this month?
- How much did I decrease my debt this month?

Physical Questions

- How much do I weigh?
- What are my cholesterol and blood pressure?
- What are my measurements?
- What is my energy level?

Then, let's get even deeper...

- Am I tracking my caloric intake?
- Do I know what the good health markers are for my age?
- Are my measurements bigger or smaller than last year? What trend does that put me on?
- What do I need to do to increase my energy?

Are these making sense? Okay, now write *your* questions down.

'P' IS FOR PLAN

Write Your Plan

My daughter took me to this cool, modern art/Instagram museum. In one of the rooms, they had all these dots on the wall. They didn't make any sense. Then, a special light came on and revealed numbers. I could start connecting the dots to form a picture. Ooooh... ahhhhh! It started to all make sense.

Once you decide what you need to do, and the order you need to do it in, you can begin to see things happen in your life. You can't go anywhere without a plan. Goals without plans are just dreams—and dreams are hard to remember when you wake up. Our plan has to make so much sense that, as we start to execute it, even other people can see where we're going.

Taking time to make an Action Plan is clearly worth every minute. Has this ever happened to you? You told your staff, or your kids, what you wanted them to do—what you wanted to happen, how you wanted them to do it, and when you wanted it completed. Then, you went on your busy way to do the things they aren't yet able to accomplish. You came back and, much to your surprise, the whole thing had gone completely off course—or even worse—*it was not done at all*!

How Does That Happen?

Most often, the problem is in the explanation.

We take for granted that people understand what we're thinking. Beyond that, we actually think *we* know what we're thinking. Huh? Yep. We often leap before we look and launch off into our future without fully planning the route to get there. Have you ever given someone what you thought were clear and concise directions, only to be met with half a dozen fantastic questions—information you really should have given them to begin with? And what's worse… you have to *think* to come up with the answers, because you now realize (on the spot) that you hadn't really thought those things through.

If you think that *maybe* I'm talking to everyone but you, prove me wrong: pull out your written goals right now.

Take Some Time: Make a Plan to Get There

You need to write your plan in pencil, because it may change a dozen times—and that's okay! We need a well-thought-out plan in order to launch out toward our goals; then, our Action Plans may need adjusting as we walk them out.

When we were building and renovating our new church property, we had detailed architectural plans before we ever broke ground. Those plans changed almost weekly. As I walked through and details slipped past me, or as things took shape and we thought there might be a better way than what was beginning to emerge, we made changes. But we could never have started the process, gotten buy-in, developed a timeline, counted the cost, or allocated resources without months of planning.

> *"If you don't design your own life plan, chances are you'll fall into someone else's plan. And guess what they have planned for you? Not much."*
> —Jim Rohn

Now, It's Your Turn

In goal-setting, we reach for the stars. In planning, we try to figure out how to get there. Write down everything you can think of that you'll need to reach your goal.

Some places to start may be:

- Will you need to research?
- Where? For how long?
- Alone? Should you reach out? To whom?

What other questions should you be asking?

If we know where we're starting from, and where we want to go, we can build our Action Plan to get there. So let's go back to the weight loss thing (which I know doesn't make any of us happy now, but can thrill us later). Before we order the extra-large and supersize the fries, if we know what we weigh each day and what we want to weigh by the end of the year, we can figure out how many pounds we have to lose.

Each pound is about 3,500 calories. We want to lose 10 pounds? 10 x 3,500 = 35,000 calories this year. We need to lose about a pound (or 3,000 calories) each month. How many calories do we need to take off every single week, or burn every day, so that we don't end up missing our goal at the end of the year?

We need to shave 3,000 calories a month off of our diet.

Okay, that means I'm going to have to cut 100 calories a day out of my food budget. What does that look like? Is that a soda? Is that a Starbucks drink? (I know saying "cutting out a Starbucks drink" is like a cuss word. Forgive me for saying that!) Pick a plan.

A little pain today is worth a lot of gain tomorrow.

What's your pathway to success? Is it exchanging a sausage biscuit for yogurt? Is it not getting the fries with that? Is it committing to 100 calories worth of exercise every day, no matter how you get it? What's your thing? Do *that!* Break it down to something small, and you'll realize, "I can do that and reach my goal!"

If you want to read more books, how many books do you want to read? If it's 12 books a year, that's just one book a month. If it's one book a month, you only need to read a quarter of a book every week. Maybe that breaks down to only two chapters every day. This way, you can keep track of your goals as you go. The difference between you and most people is that most people have a dream they'll never figure out how to accomplish.

Let's say your dream is to write a book. That's a pretty big undertaking. Let me ask you this question: Have you started writing anything? If you want to write a book, what are the steps you need to take to get there? Let's assess where you are. "Well, I don't know my writing voice." How are you going to change that? Are you going to start journaling every day? Are you going to start a blog and post three times a week? Are you going to contact a publisher? Are you going to reach out to a book agent? Are you going to research what it takes to write a book proposal? For each of these things that we want to do, let's measure and assess so we know how to get there.

Let's build an action plan.

What's your dream? What will it take to get to your dream? Now, what we're going to do is print it. We're going to write it down.

Once we *measure* (M) where we are today and *assess* (A) what's going on, we can begin to *plan* (P) our action steps to get there. Write down that Action Plan. Writing it down (not typing it) physically engages us in the process and embeds it more deeply into our memory.

Are you going to Get On It? You've got to plan to work and then work the plan. You whine, "But I've had goals before and they didn't work out." You didn't do this step. No plan, no work. *The difference between effectiveness and busyness is whether you're willing to follow through with your plan.*

Let's Get On It and get effective.

GET GOING - DEEP

> *"A wise man thinks ahead; a fool doesn't*
> *and even brags about it!"*
> —Proverbs 13:16, TLB

Let's stop thinking about it and *do* it. Faith words without faith actions are dead. Let's move, people! You can't let your dream die now!

The question is, "How can I… (list your goals)?"

Now, write down 10-20 strategies for *each* goal and attach deadlines. You should have a comprehensive collection of ideas, ranging from the obviously mundane to the wild and borderline crazy, for every goal. Don't forget to *stretch* your imagination!

- Break it down: What is your plan? What are the steps to get there?
- Practical steps: *Attach a plan to the goal!*
- Write the steps you are going to take and attach deadlines

An indicator of how successful you'll be this year is how quickly you take action. How much time will it take you to get moving? Are you point-and-shoot? Or do you need to consider it for a couple of weeks before you begin? *Studies indicate that your success is in direct correlation to how quickly you take action.* You might be disappointed in yourself. *Stop it,* and *just move on!*

Pick up that pen! Take action, now!

Quit Talking About Someday

Someday ain't on the calendar (bad grammar, good premise). You can't do anything about yesterday, but you are in complete control of where you go today. So, let's change our direction, which ultimately changes our destination! Success, here we come!

> *"I have been impressed with the urgency of doing. Knowing is not enough; we must apply. Being willing is not enough; we must do."*
> —Leonardo da Vinci

We're going to plan for tomorrow, today. Preparation is the difference-maker.

I usually meet with my assistant on Mondays. We review the whole week so I know what's coming and I can start planning for success. Then, every night, she sends me my agenda for the next day. That allows me to set my alarm clock for the right time, plan my wardrobe and set out what I'm going to need to succeed so that I don't run out of the house without it. It allows me time to ponder my upcoming day, in case I get an idea or inspiration.

Just a little planning can go a *long* way!

WRITE IT AGAIN, SAM

Let's write our action plan every day for 30 days.

As a matter of fact, you can go back to that tool that I gave away free on my website, *NicoleCrank.com.* You can print those downloadable worksheets and fill them in every day for 30 days. Don't look back. Just look at what's happening *today.*

Just keep trying to stretch your brain. You might forget some pieces. You might forget some steps. As you recall and write it for 30 days, it's going to get ingrained into your heart. It's going to be on your mind. It's going to infiltrate your spirit. It's going to give you the steps you need to get to the end of the year and say, "Look at what I've done."

You're writing 7-10 goals. You're getting a vision for them. You're keeping them out in front of you. You're writing an Action Plan for each goal and you're reading it out loud daily. A big part of action is *saying.* Say it, then do it. Saying it helps propel us to do it! What are you going to say every day that aligns with the *vision* you see?

Say your goals out loud (the way you wrote them, specifically, and in the present tense). Say your Action Plan out loud—the plan to meet at least one of your goals every day. You reinforce what you repeat.

When you hear something, you have a tendency to believe it. But do you know who you believe more than any other person on the planet? *You!* When you say something, you believe it on a deeper level than if any other person on the planet had said it. When you say it, your reticulating activator, the part of your brain that controls systems like breathing and blinking your eyes (neither of which you were thinking about before I mentioned them) does its best to make the things that you say come to pass. Intentionally say the things about your future that you want!

Personally, I think declaring my fitness goals out loud holds me more accountable. I've found that much more difficult to do when my mouth is full of chocolate chip cookies! Unfortunately, that's an example of my actions not matching up with my words. If we honestly expect to reach our goals, our actions have to line up with what our mouths are declaring. Most of the time, our actions do speak *way* louder than our words. So we have to ask ourselves: "What have my *actions* been saying?"

> *"Dear friends, do you think you'll get anywhere in this if you learn all the right words but never do anything?"*
> –James 2:14 (MSG)

"The most effective way to do it, is to do it."
—Amelia Earhart

Step Four:
GET RESULTS: THE BENEFITS OF COMMITMENT

HERE'S WHERE THE POWER IS

> *"If you set goals and go after them with all the determination you can muster, your gifts will take you places that will amaze you."*
> —Les Brown

Did you know there's immense power in simply NOT quitting, not giving up, staying in the game and fighting through the last round? Still pushing forward, even when you don't see things changing—that's commitment!

I know some people are a little nervous about getting married because it seems like a huge commitment. People don't like to sign long-term contracts for the same reason. Yet here I am talking to you about commitment. Don't freak out. Don't be afraid. It's going to be alright. As a matter of fact, I have faith that you won't give up on your dreams when the going gets tough. Did you know there are a lot of rewards that come with commitment? (Hmmmm. Rewards? Yup. Does that make you feel better?)

I heard a story when I was in college about a professor who taught a really hard class. Everyone in his class had a lot of homework and projects; but he kept telling his students, "You're going to be really glad you did it. You're going to be proud of yourself, if you turn this in."

Everyone in the class did their homework. Every single person in the class did their projects. It was unbelievable. The weeks passed, and it came to final exam day. As the professor got ready to hand out the final exams, he said, "If you don't want to take this test, you don't have to. I have a deal for you, because you did the homework. You stayed in the game when it looked hard. Because you turned in all your projects without missing one, I will give you an automatic C." Who wouldn't want *that* in college? I think it was an urban legend in the making!

The professor continued, "Anybody who wants to stay will have an opportunity to make a better grade than that." One by one, the students started getting up, dodging the professor's gaze and darting out of the room. Everybody wanted in on that deal. Eventually, less than half the class remained in the room. I guess the commitment was too scary.

If you can get away with a C without doing the work, you'd probably think, "I'll take those bones." But who wants bones when you can have steak, right? We have to start thinking about the rewards that come with hanging in there—and how we can do so.

The professor passed out the tests, facedown, and said, "Everybody, this is a timed test. No one look. At the exact same time, everyone can turn it over. I just want to tell you that I'm really proud of you for believing in yourself, for studying, for working hard and for not taking the easy way out."

It's easy to get off the road at any point. Don't do it. Don't give up. There's power in simply not quitting.

He kept affirming them and telling them how proud he was, how excited he was. Then, he said, "Now turn your test over." On the first line, it said,

> *"I'm so proud of you for not quitting, for believing in yourself, and for this... today, you get an automatic A."*

I wonder how many times in life we've been living with the Cs when an A was just a few more steps away. I want that A+ life. So how do we get it? Commitment!

Maybe we need a little help remembering not to quit. We can certainly take advantage of the technology at our fingertips: "Alexa, set a reminder for tomorrow at 9:00 AM to remind me to *go get* my goals." In fact, why don't you pull your phone out right now and set daily, weekly, and monthly reminders? Don't wait. That's the execution part we talked about. Why put off until later (and likely forget) what we can do right now?

Let's get our goals out.

Look at them again. Get ready. Review them one more time. Keep that *focus*. Keep that motivation, even while you're doing other things.

What Motivates You?

Ask yourself, "*Why* am I doing what I'm doing?"

Write this answer down, and use that answer as a means to stay determined. You see, a lot of people give up on their goals because they've lost or misplaced their motivation.

For me, the best way to stay committed is to keep my motivation in front of me. I'll print a photo of myself from when I was ten pounds heavier than I am now, and post it somewhere visible in my workout area to remind me that this (*ugh!*) is what I'll get if I don't exercise. Then, I'll post a photo of what I looked like at my best (or a photo of someone else I'm working toward). The difference-maker is only 30 minutes of effort a day. I can do that!

Sometimes, it's so hard for me to put one foot in front of the other when it comes to walking on my treadmill. But those are steps I need to take in order to keep myself in good health. When I feel the burn, I'm feeling the fat cells dying (it's their cry for help—Help! I'm melting! LOL.) and the Goal-Getting Me emerging!

We're all moving toward somewhere. Which way are you headed? Even if you've been distracted, or wandered completely off the path, you can turn around and start putting one foot in front of the other. That's all it takes to get back on track. I *know* you can do it! You're going to make it!

> "*The first step towards getting somewhere is to decide that you are not going to stay where you are.*"
> —Chauncey Depew (U.S. Senator, 1899-1911)

Here's another thing to remember: don't punish yourself for stopping. Celebrate the fact that you're starting again. After all, that *is* the definition of success: getting up one more time than you fall down! The prize doesn't always go to the most talented, the fastest or the most privileged. Usually, it goes to the person who just *won't quit!*

I want you to make me say, "They just don't have any quittin' sense!" as you're finishing that manuscript, buying that outfit you've been eyeing in the smaller size, telling me about your wedding plans, or buying that new car. Commitment can get you all of those things!

Take action, now!

Don't let this moment pass you by. Over the years, I've seen many people search for that one big, life-changing miracle or sign. *Often, the matrix of our miracle is not in some mighty and marvelous moment or singular occurrence; it's in these seemingly insignificant, daily steps.* These are the steps that lead to your miracle. So what are you waiting for?

Are the steps you're taking today drawing you *closer to* or leading you further away from your goals?

COMMITMENT PAYS WHEN THERE SEEMS TO BE NO WAY

Monday isn't most people's favorite day of the week… but everyone loves payday! You've got to do the work to get the pay. I want to help keep you motivated to see your goals through to the end. Are you going to be one of the 25% who give up on their resolutions in the first week? I don't think so. You've already passed that. You're already in the top 75%. Or maybe you're in with 60% who give up on their dream in just six months. Have 180 days whipped you? *No!* Not you! The difference is that you and I are walking through the whole program together.

I want to remind you who you are and how far you've already come. In our *First Step*, you got your goals on paper. Yay! By writing them down, you're already in the top 3%. *Boom!* Feel that momentum? By getting them down in ink, you became 42% closer to accomplishing your goals than all the other people. Some other folks in your office may want that promotion, but you're doing what it takes to *get* it. A few of your friends are daydreaming about that summer body they want, but you're visualizing and hustling to make it happen.

That brings us to the *Second Step* we did: we came up with our *vision* to keep it before us. You've got to see it to be it! Then, you internalized it by writing your goals for 30 days. It's not a random dream, but something you carry deep in your heart.

Next, we talked about the MAP of *action*. M.A.P. was an acronym: steps we can walk through to get us to the clear destination we're headed toward—with gusto!

And now, *commitment* That reminds me of a true story about Notre Dame…

There Was a Child Named Montana

Montana had a terminal brain tumor. They asked him, "What's the one thing that you want?"

Montana said, "I'd love to visit with a player from the Notre Dame football team." He got more than he expected. A player didn't just stop by; the head coach himself made the trip. Coach Weiss walked into the room and went straight to Montana's bedside to spend some quality time with him.

The athletic little boy had lost the use of his lower extremities—he couldn't even get out of bed. Still, he managed to throw a pass, with just one hand, to the coach in the living room of his home. The coach asked, "What's one thing I can do for you?"

Montana said, "I'd like to call a play."

The coach said, "It's yours!"

Montana said, "On the first offensive play of the game next week, I want you to pass to the right."

Coach said, "Wow, that's very specific. But all right. I'll do it."

It was a big commitment: if the score turned out to be close, the outcome of the whole game could have rested on this one decision. Montana only lived another day-and-a-half. His mama held him as he passed on to glory. That week, the family honored Montana's memory by watching the football team that he loved.

Sure enough, on the first play from scrimmage, Notre Dame was backed up on their own one yard line. Things could really go badly from here.

The players said, "Coach, what's the play?"

He looked at them and said, "You know what the play is. It's Montana's play. We're going to pass it to the right."

They said, "No, that's not gonna work."

The family watching at home said, "Oh, there's no way they can run Montana's play. They're not going to do it. Not in this kind of situation." But sure enough, the committed Coach Weiss kept his word. When they passed to the right, the other team was *so* not expecting it!

Not only did they not get scored on—they got a first down out of the play!

So many times, it seems like we just can't do it. We can't make that happen. But it says in the Bible to take your vision, write it down, and now... *run* with it! (Montana would be so proud of you!)

We talked about this in our Goal-Setting and Vision Steps. Then, we worked that MAP from Step Three and made our Action Plan all based on Habakkuk 2:2. Now, the next verse leads us to Step Four of Getting Gains through commitment. The wisest book in the world says,

*"For still the vision awaits its appointed time; it
hastens to the end—it will not lie. If it seems slow,
wait for it; it will surely come; it will not delay."*
—Habakkuk 2:3 (ESV)

You might be thinking, *"Nicole, I don't know if I can make it
through this! It's taking so long! It's getting hard! I'm not seeing
anything happen!"*

This is something I want you to write down: *If it seems slow…
wait for it. It will surely come. It will not delay. It's on the way!* I
know God's working for you behind the scenes, right now. He's
making a way where there seems to be no way.

"I can do all things through Christ who strengthens me."
—Philippians 4:13 (NKJV)

God has big plans for you. They're for good and not for evil—to
bring you to an expected end. It wasn't your plan to begin with;
it was God's plan that He put on the inside of you! God's plans
never fail. Stay committed. You *can* see it through!

There is so much power in simply not quitting!

ACHIEVING: WHICH FROG ARE YOU?

This is a transition step from doing what it takes to *start* and doing what it takes to *achieve. Motivation gets you started; commitment delivers the package.*

We're always moving toward something. We're developing habits every single day, whether intentionally or unintentionally. Unintentionally, we may be hitting the snooze button three times, moving too slowly, and needing that first cup of coffee to get us going. Then, we dash through traffic to work because we're running late. Or, instead, we can decide to become intentional with our lives. *Successful people do what unsuccessful people are not willing to do: continue to make those hard (in the moment) choices that you won't see the results of for some time.*

I remember hearing the story of two frogs that fell into a bucket of cream. At first, they thought their dreams had come true, and they drank their fill of the best creamy stuff they'd ever tasted. They were grinning because they were more full than they'd ever been… until they looked around and realized that they were trapped. The sides of the dairy bucket were too tall for them to hop out and too slick for them to climb out.

Their dream had become their last meal.

The frogs had been treading milk the whole time they were drinking, and they knew they couldn't last much longer. The realization hit them hard. Depression and despair started to set in. They yelled for an hour as they swam and got more and more exhausted.

One frog finally made a fatal decision. "It's hopeless. We're doomed. We should just give up, die with dignity, and quit yelling and screaming." With that, he sunk into the cream and died. The other frog wasn't ready to give up just yet. He swam in circle after circle and continued yelling, with no results. The words of the other frog started to haunt him. "It's hopeless," he heard over and over.

Exhausted, unable to continue, he stopped for a moment and expected to sink. Instead, his foot hit something solid. They had kicked so long and so hard that the cream had turned into butter. The frog used his last ounce of strength to push off from the butter he'd churned and jump out of the bucket. His commitment to continue when it didn't look good saved him.

> *"I have not failed. I've simply discovered*
> *10,000 ways that don't work."*
> —Thomas Edison

Successful people fail their way to the top. They choose not to quit. They decide to make it happen. *They don't break down before they break through.* The road to success may include 10,000 ways that didn't work in order to find that one way that does.

Focus 5

Distraction is another thing that keeps us from reaching our goals. We need the ability to pull our focus back. When life gets blurry, adjust your focus. We might get short on time. "Urgent" things might pop up: an illness, a big project, relationship stress, or boredom might creep in. What do we do? We can give up or *get* up.

I want you to *write*:

- Five reasons you won't give up
- Five ways you will get up one more time
- Five incentives to stay the course

Things will always have the opportunity to get derailed. You will fail, gain some weight, spend some money, or blow your top. But make a decision to fail forward—to *fail your way to success*. That way, you'll already know exactly what *not* to do.

Write this (or your own version of it—let it flow!)

This is my declaration:

I can do this!
I can do this today!
I can do this well!

And tomorrow, I will do it again... a little bit better.

Now, say it out loud. You believe what you say!

It's the small things no one sees that create the results everyone wants. Discipline closes the gap between what you want and what you actually achieve. It's the bridge between who you are and who you want to become.

> *"Thou shalt decree a thing and it will be established."*
> —Job 22:28

IT'S YOUR CHOICE: WHICH PAIN DO YOU PREFER?

There's no such thing as a pain-free life. But sometimes, we can choose our pain; and in the opinion of most, there's one pain that's much more bearable than any other. There's the pain of discipline, and there's the pain of regret. Which do you prefer?

Being disciplined is hard, but living in regret is much worse. Based on who you want to be, ask yourself, "What kind of discipline do I need to start?" *Discipline allows us to collect on the compound interest of the pain of today.*

Compound interest was called the eighth wonder of the world by Albert Einstein, because what it can do is almost magical. Small deposits, made right away, yield almost unbelievable results, over time! The habits, routines, strides, effort, and work we put in today can yield results we would never think possible!

It works for our benefit (for better or worse) in our careers, our marriages, and every other area of our lives. Inch by inch… it's a cinch!

Little steps (thoughtfulness) compounded
Tiny tweaks (compromise) compounded
Time/Patience (civility) compounded

For Better:

- Giving up 100 calories a day compounded = losing 10½ pounds a year!
- Going to the gym just two times a week compounded = great muscle mass and strength gained!
- One date night a week compounded = a deeper and more fulfilling relationship, a long, happy marriage… your preferred future, amplified!

For Worse:

- Eating terribly because of stress compounded = gaining 10½ pounds a year! Ugh!
- No exercise because we "can't" find the time compounded = that "dad bod" or "mom bod" we never thought we'd have…ever!
- No affection/affirmation in our marriage—compounded = Suddenly, an affair or divorce yields a future we never wanted to encounter.

You may not see the results today, tomorrow or even next year. But they'll be worth the wait!

> *"Success doesn't come from what you do occasionally.*
> *It comes from what you do consistently."*
> —Marie Forleo

WHEN COMMITMENT LEADS TO GETTING GAINS: SUDDENLY

There is a delicate plant that yields beautiful, purple-blue (and sometimes pink) flowers with six petals. They can be really pretty! But if you try to grow them, you might get discouraged. Don't quit just because the thing you want doesn't blossom quickly enough.

The water hyacinth can be like our goals and dreams: elusive. We see a big pond of possibility and water (opportunity) as far as the eye can see. One lonely water hyacinth (your goal) sits there…and nothing seems to be happening. Day 1, Day 8, Day 14, Day 18, Day 25, Day 29… After a while, it seems like we should just walk away. Everything we did to grow the hyacinth doesn't seem to have worked.

What we can't see is that this plant grows by colonization. It sends out short runners, below the surface, that create all of these daughter plants. What you can't see about reaching your goals is that the daily writing, internalizing, visualization, and commitment is really sending out roots. On Day 29, one half of the pond's surface will be open water. On the 30th day, *suddenly*, the entire pond will be covered by a blanket of beautiful water hyacinths.

You will not see any water at all! It's pretty amazing!

Just because you've been working your tail off and not seeing results, yet, doesn't mean you should walk away. The gains are coming. The only way out is through. (I have a talk on YouTube called "Don't Ring That Bell"—you should watch it!) Don't give up! By the time you finally see the results, the process will probably be so far along that the surface of the pond (the scope of your dreams) will be covered.

Your "suddenly" might be a year away… but it'll be worth it!

Good Things Come to Those Who Wait

Your "suddenly" might seem like something that should surprise you. But it comes day by day, call by call, sale by sale, and penny by penny. My father-in-law used to have a saying about doing things consistently, the right way. He said, "It might look like you're going slower… but you're really going faster."

When I was younger, I made a lot of money in the corporate world and met my goal of retiring by age 30. By then, I'd made enough that I could afford to volunteer full-time. I was able to spend my time pouring into the needs of people through our church. The church couldn't afford to put me on salary, and I didn't expect it. I just did whatever was needed. I didn't give up when I didn't get to do what I wanted. I didn't quit when I got bored. I didn't walk away when no one offered me a job. I just did what I knew I was supposed to do.

One year turned into two. I didn't win any sales awards, get my name called at the big meetings, go out for congratulatory dinners, or head off on any exotic president's club trips. I just kept volunteering. Two years turned into three. Getting to use the corporate jet to bring clients to corporate headquarters to meet with CIOs or CEOs in boardrooms was beginning to be a distant memory. Three years turned into four. I'm giving you the details because my "suddenly" took four years, and a little more.

Don't get weary in well-doing. Your efforts are going to catch up with you with compound interest.

In year four, my husband and I "suddenly" became senior pastors of a church. I didn't realize much change in my own life, except that I actually came on staff. (I finally had a salary that wasn't a whole heck of a lot more than minimum wage.) I still did whatever needed to be done; our church began to grow. I filled the role of executive pastor as we grew from 180 people to 2,000 in about two years. My husband asked me to start speaking occasionally, and I began a women's ministry and conference.

Then, we started another church campus across town (before we'd ever heard of such a thing), grew over 100% that year, and inadvertently became multi-campus model pioneers. My first conference sold out, and we launched monthly women's events. Our church outgrew its existing location, and we got a building over three times as large. Next, we started another campus in St. Louis and our first campus in Florida. I began speaking every weekend in one of the two states.

Today, we have four campuses in St. Louis, two campuses in Florida, and I've been given a television show that has grown to an international platform, including the U.S., Africa and Europe! This is my third book, and I have another one about to release next year.

I left a big income and went to no income for four years. Yet God was meeting my every need, want, and desire. I finally moved "up" to a small income with the intention to stay committed to the cause…whatever was needed. If we keep working in the present, God is busy in the future, opening doors and honoring our faithfulness.

I only share this to encourage you to *stay the course!* God and your faithfulness are going to catch up to you in ways that are going to blow you away! You can do this!

> *"Commit to the Lord whatever you do, and*
> *he will establish your plans."*
> —Proverbs 16:3

YOU'LL ONLY CONQUER WHAT YOU'RE WILLING TO COMMIT TO

Don't tell your momma I said this, but I'm giving you permission to be stubborn as a mule.

A farmer had a mule that was sick and injured. The vet gave the farmer the bad news: his mule wasn't going to make it. The farmer knew the mule wouldn't live long, but he couldn't bring himself to shoot it. So he put the mule in the bottom of a deep hole to bury him. It would only be a matter of time.

The farmer didn't know how to fill the hole in, so he decided to start dumping his trash in there. For a couple of days, it looked like his plan was going to work. However, a few days later, the mule was shaking off the trash and trying to stand up. Every time the farmer went to the hole to dump in his trash, he'd find the mule standing on top of it. It got to the point that the farmer would pour out his garbage and the mule would just *shake* it off, *eat* the good parts, and *stomp* the rest of the junk beneath his feet.

Soon, the mule started looking healthier and stronger; but the farmer had no idea how to get him out. His fate had already been decided. The mule would have to die in the deep hole (of depression, bankruptcy, sickness, and betrayal). Except that the Missouri mule didn't give up. All he had was the trash to live on, but live on it he did. He ate what he could and stood on the rest. As the days passed, and even more people's junk was dumped on top of him, he started rising higher and higher. It took a few months; but eventually, the Missouri mule walked himself right out of the hole that was meant to be his grave!

Be as committed to your dream as a Missouri mule. Endure the pitiful looks. Don't give up when they say the prognosis is bad. Commitment is not quitting just because it looks like the deal died. Lazarus died, but it wasn't over! He was raised from the dead!

Dead dreams can be resurrected, too.

Doctors told me I had stage four cancer, and that I'd probably never be able to have more children. But my daughter, Ashtyn, is a happy, healthy teenager! (David and I just kept trying.) The bank said they wouldn't loan *that* amount of money to us for an investment on a property, but they later changed their minds, and we got the money! I was rocked when someone sold a piece of land for an amount I couldn't afford and then rubbed it in my face. But I ended up owning it for *under* my original offer price.

Just because they told you *no*...
Just because it gets *hard*…
Just because it takes *longer*…
Just because the plan had a twist you didn't see…
…doesn't mean you have to quit.

The decision you have to make is this: Do you still want it, and does God still want you to have it?

You have two choices:

1) Quit now and seal the deal: you ain't ever gonna get it.

   or

2) Look at what just happened and shake it off like a Missouri mule. Keep on going! I was raised in St. Louis, and Missouri mules have a reputation for being stubborn. That isn't *always* a bad thing!

Our dreams may be so big that they seem like gigantic elephants to us. But we know there's only one way to eat an elephant, and that's *one bite-at-a-time!*

EXECUTION — (THE GOOD KIND)

Execution means doing it when it's easy and not quitting when it's hard. The execution of your commitment includes… well, it's a four-letter word. I'm not sure I should write a four-letter word in print, but here goes… Execution is W-O-R-K. Execution is doing the do. It's not getting distracted. It's where the rubber meets the road. The enemy can plan your distraction, but he cannot plan your destruction. He will try to distract you with every little thing; but we have to stay glued to our plan of execution.

God doesn't tell us to be strong and courageous because life is like Disney World. He tells us to be strong and courageous because it's going to take strength and courage to get where we're supposed to go. That's why faith is such an integral part of success. There are so many potential stops along the way—so many places we can step out of the game and let some second-string player step into the destiny that God created specifically for us, while we sit on the bench and *catch our breath*. The key to finishing our race is never quitting—continuing to put one foot in front of the other, even if it looks like we might not win. A guaranteed way to lose is to quit.

"But that sounds hard, and I don't think it's biblical," you say.

Oh really? If you want to look up execution in the Bible, that's probably not the word you should search. The Bible uses the word "diligence." Take a look:

> *"For this very reason, adding your diligence [to the divine promises], employ every effort in exercising your faith to develop virtue (excellence, resolution, Christian energy), and in [exercising] virtue [develop] knowledge (intelligence)."*
> —2 Peter 1:5 (AMP)

Thinking faith thoughts, speaking faith words, and execution—where faith words turn into faith actions—empower you to walk out that desire, dream, business, calling, plan... that *thing* that God has put inside of you. *God doesn't do what He can do until we do everything we can do.* To multiply what God has invested in you, (His love, His son, creation, breath, talent, gifts, plans, purpose) you have to fully execute. The great Coach

Vince Lombardi said, "You'll either have reasons or you'll have results. Which one do you want?"

I was a cheerleader in high school. (Hmmm… does that make me qualified to say this?) Use this book as your push to succeed…your personal pep rally… your inspiration to get out of the stands and into the game! Use this as your reason to step out in faith and fulfill your destiny! *Go! Go execute!* You can *do it!* I'm cheering for you!

I've always loved to sing. I sing in the bathroom with my daughter. I'm not bad… but I'm not good, either. I won the lead in my high school musical, which gave me the opportunity to perform in my little town's arena. But it never went anywhere. I always wondered if there was anything I should have done with my singing.

Today, I think I've figured it out.

I would sing with my daughter when she was little (who is *so* much more talented than me). I realize now how my gift and love for singing motivated her to execute and become better. I sang to her when she was a baby in the rocking chair. I sang to her when she was a toddler in the bathtub. We sang about every little activity we did, and made up songs about everything. What I did wasn't about me. My small gift was there so I could encourage *her* to practice, develop, grow and not give up on her incredible gift. Everyone needs someone cheering them on to bring out the best of their God-given talents. That's my job... I'm her biggest fan!

I want to do the same thing for you. Let's go! What's the first thing you're going to do today to start executing your plan? Because it's going to take some practice to get good at it.

PRACTICE MAKES PERFECT

It's been said that, in order to become truly excellent at anything, you have to either spend 10 years or 10,000 hours working at it. So, if you want to be a singer, you'd better sing day and night in order to make it before you're 30.

Take professional athletes, for example. Pro basketball players didn't start playing in college. No, they were the kids who played every night after school until dark. They never quit. They honed their gifts until they were good enough for people to take notice. They played when they wanted to and they practiced when they absolutely did *not* want to. Who wants to do 100 free throws in a row every day for five days after you've been playing for ten years? Michael Jordan. There's a reason he is who he is!

Once we've identified our goals based on our giftings (whether it's singing, basketball, business, inventing, writing, organization, caring for children—whatever it is), we need to start using it all the time. We need to plan for it. We need to work that plan and not give up on it. We need to execute the plan. We all want to be noticed for something. We shouldn't think we'll be recognized if we've only been practicing for a year. That's not how it works. Remember, it takes 10,000 hours (even if you're naturally talented) to hone your skill, understand it, work it, and know how to overcome the relevant obstacles without letting others see you sweat… it takes time to flow in your calling—to become excellent in it.

Give it some time. Do your thing. Do it well. And do it as much as you can.

Every hour you spend using the gift God has given you puts you one hour closer to becoming truly excellent in it. You'll be one hour closer to fulfilling the destiny God has for you. How have you seen practice, diligence, or time spent working on a gifting make a difference in your life?

Now, quit reading this and go practice. *That's* commitment!

FEEL THE BURN!

In 1519, Hernán Cortés was the first Spanish explorer to land in Mexico. He brought 553 soldiers and 11 ships. You'd think that would be enough to invade and conquer a country.

However, they realized that they were up against over five million inhabitants.

The odds were roughly one soldier to every 7,500 natives… and some change. Not good. But their orders were to take the land. When his men saw what they were up against, they got scared and wanted to go home. So, Cortés gave the command: *"Burn all the ships!"* No Plan B. Total commitment. No turning back now!

Nine times out of ten, people opt out, not when circumstances *get* hard, but when things begin to *look like* they could get hard.

Read that line again out loud.

The enemy is a liar! He wants you to say "no" to the opportunity. He wants you to stay stuck where you've been.

> *"There's a difference between interest and commitment. When you're interested in doing something, you do it only when it's convenient. When you're committed to something, you accept no excuses; only results."*
> —Kenneth Blanchard

Earlier, I told you about leaving my job in corporate sales in 1999. That was in the days of dial-up internet connectivity when sales leads were on paper. I had this box of leads written on 3x5 index cards. It was a virtual goldmine! On each card, I'd written down the company name, contact person, phone number, email, when their contract was up, how much money they were worth, and the kind of business they did.

All these people *wanted* to do business with me, but they were still in a contract that hadn't expired. I knew all their renewal dates, and my future was looking pretty good! My sales funnel was *stacked* with warm leads. When God told me to quit my job, I wasn't sure how that was going to go over with my husband. I made a *lot* of money. When I told him, "Baby, I think I'm supposed to quit my job," he said, "I've been waiting for you to tell me that, because I think you're supposed to quit your job, too."

When I gave up my high-paying job to volunteer at the church, I put my golden box of sales leads up on the shelf in our closet, where it would be nice and safe. *After all, you I never know if this church thing will work out. I might need it again some day.* Then, one day, while I was praying, God began talking to me about that file box. He said, "Why do you need to keep that in your closet?"

"I dunno," I responded, playing dumb with myself and God (Note: that doesn't work). "*Maybe I'll sell it one day. Yeah. That's what I'll do."*

God said, "You're going to burn those leads." Well, that didn't make any sense. "Nicole, I want you to go to the backyard, I want you to start a fire and I want you to burn all those leads."

I didn't want to. I pouted. I doubted. I came up with a dozen reasons why these cards being in the closet was a great idea. But I knew they were my way back into a business I was supposed to be out of now. So I walked out to the back yard with some matches and lighter fluid. I had to stand out there and watch probably hundreds of thousands of dollars' worth of irreplaceable information burn to ashes! Total commitment.

"No turning back. "Nicole. You work for Me now." Burn all the ships!

Do you have something in your life that God wants you to let go of and burn up in order to move forward? (Got matches?)

GET THE RIGHT CIRCLE OF FRIENDS: RIGHT PEOPLE, RIGHT RESULTS

Our goals aren't just about getting there…they're about staying there. Little by little, inch by inch, one step at a time, we listen, learn, improve and increase in knowledge, strength and character. Getting the right mentorship (like my Circle of Friends) is a game changer.

Don't tell your goals to people who want to push you down. Tell that person who's not going to let you quit when things get hard—who's going to lift you up, believe in you, and pray for you. Share with a person who's trustworthy, who's going to keep you accountable when it's fun *and* when it just feels like work. Be intentional about finding at least one person who can celebrate where you're going and challenge you to *keep* going. Identify those groups of people who motivate you and sharpen your iron. It's more important than you think.

I've read many times that we are the sum total of the five people with whom we spend the most time. Median income, relationship status, hobbies, attitude, motivation, and more get averaged from those five. So, who are the five in your life?

Many of these people are probably already around you, and they're not threatened by the fact that you're on your way. As a matter of fact, they're probably trying to help you. Those are the people you want to pray with you; those are the ones who will challenge and encourage you. It's safe to share with them. They won't roll over and tell you what you want to hear; but they will be courteous about your feelings.

Everyone is called to hold a hand up to someone who is where they want to go, but also hold a hand down to someone trying to get where you are.

That makes the best circle—one in which we can all learn from each other. *It can't be all about you. You need to pour out so there's more room for someone else to pour in.*

This is why you need an accountability partner. You need someone verbally authorized to let you know when you start sandbagging. You need a friend who loves you so much that they'll come alongside you on the hard days and who will break their diet to eat fried ice cream with you on celebration days. You need that encouragement!

The Bible says that, when you go on a fast, you're not supposed to brag about it. But when I go on a fast, I do tell my family. It's not as a bragging point, but more as a way of staying accountable. That way, they won't tempt me or look at me funny if I refuse to go for ice cream! If I'm only supposed to have one cup of coffee a day, and they know that, they can help remind me and keep me honest if I forget. My kids will say, "Mom, didn't you already have coffee today?"

Your accountability partner can help guide you with just a little positive pressure: "Stay on your goal!" Those are the kind of people you want to have your back. Surround yourself with quality people. Show me your friends and I'll show you your future! Not all of these people have to be folks you actually sit down with, face to face. I've been personally coached by the greatest of the great: Tony Robbins, John Maxwell, Patrick Lencioni, and so many more. Most of these people, I've only had the pleasure of meeting face to face once or twice; but I regularly meet with them in my bathroom.

What do I mean by that?

When I'm getting ready in the morning, I'm not wasting my time. They talk (via coaching series, Circle of Friends, audiobook, YouTube video, podcast, and more) and I listen. I already know what I know. I need to know what *they* know. I want them to be part of my top five.

Who do you want to be part of your top five influencers?

1. _____

2. _____

3. _____

4. _____

5. _____

6. _____

7. _____

I know—I put seven lines. Why? Because your circle of friends (which is the title of a partnership group I mentor and coach on a monthly basis, by exposing them to the expertise of some of my richest business and ministry relationships) isn't limited to five, or even seven. Those are both great numbers, but you might have a couple more—and if you do, I applaud you!

Commitment pays in rewards. So don't look at the trial—look at the reward. What do I get?

Step Five:

GET HAPPY! THE FUEL OF TAKING TIME TO ENJOY THE REWARD

It's time we reframe what success means, shuck the guilt for still having things on our never-ending to-do list, and party like it's 1999 over the things we've accomplished.

Why is it that the easiest thing to put off until tomorrow is celebrating the *gains* we made today?

Instead of leaving the salt mines stressed out about the salt we didn't get, what if we consider how much we *did* get done! Let's take a breath and live it up over the wins instead of being so "salty" about the things we haven't won yet. (Notice that these aren't losses—just future wins.)

How do you paint the town red and still move forward? There are a few ways, and the first one sounds like a real snoozer but is incredibly important.

GET REST

I know there's somebody out there who wants to quit their job.

But maybe you're not called to quit. Maybe all you really need is a vacation... a small reward for your work so far. What if all you need is rest so that your mind is sharp to finish the job? I know, Mr(s). Motivated—you're thinking, "I don't have time to rest." Honestly, you don't have time *not* to. (This is also the section I need to read to myself on a regular basis. Just being honest.)

You need time you can use to sharpen your axe (let me get into your "axe business" for a minute). "Sharpen your axe?" What exactly does that mean?

There's a story of two lumberjacks, back in the 1900s, who were competing for the same big job. The owner told them, "Here's the deal. I need to clear 500 acres of land. The guy who can cut down the most trees in a day gets the whole job."

The two guys grabbed their axes and went to work. The first guy skipped breakfast, worked through lunch, and took no breaks (not even a bathroom break!) He worked right through dinner, cutting down trees as fast as he could, from sun-up until sun-down. He never stopped even once, all day! He was so proud of himself, because he was certain that he'd won... especially since the second guy took multiple breaks. He'd even disappeared for a while (the first lumberjack guessed he'd taken a long bathroom break). He took a break for lunch. He stopped and ate dinner. *What's going on?* The first guy wondered. *Such a lazy loser!*

At the end of the day, the owner came back to award the business… and guess what happened? The first guy, who worked all day and never stopped, actually had *less* productivity. He had fewer trees in his pile than the guy who stopped for occasional breaks. He couldn't believe it! The second lumberjack who took all the breaks explained: "Every time I took a break, I sharpened my axe!"

That's what rest will do for you!

That's what a vacation is. That's how a few days of "staycation" can pay off. It allows all the "decision fatigue" to fall away. It means sitting still until you actually get bored. It's sleeping until you wake up naturally (and not from stress!)

It takes most people 2-3 days before they actually *start* to unwind. Then, real rest can begin. For my workaholic friends (I'm speaking to my tribe right now. You're *busted*, because I'm one of you!), a one-week vacation doesn't cut it. It takes workaholics *two* unplugged weeks to actually heal and begin to run again. Life isn't a sprint… it's a marathon. And marathon runners don't run marathons every day. Neither can you!

Run… *rest*…run again!

Stay Close to Your Center

A few years ago, we started a new family tradition. We love going to New York City to watch the Macy's Thanksgiving Day Parade. The last time we were there, we went to see the Rockettes at Radio City Music Hall. It was amazing! One of the coolest parts of the show is when they form this huge high-kicking human pinwheel and rotate it on stage… like the blades of a giant fan!

The girls at the very end of the line struggle and have to take really big steps in order to keep up. But it was interesting to me how the girls in the center barely moved at all. The closer we are to our center (our goal and purpose) the less we have to struggle. In fact, it's practically effortless! Still, those Rockettes have spent hours, days, and weeks practicing those moves to have the muscle memory to do them right when the time comes.

By stressing and not resting, we're constantly overestimating our own ability to control the situation and underestimating God's power to handle things. Most of the time, it's just dumb stuff that keeps us awake at night, anyway! *There's a huge difference between a good idea and a God idea.* I'll never forget hearing a wise man once say, "It isn't what God told me to do that almost killed me. It's what I decided to do without Him."

Keep the main thing the main thing—your God-given call and purpose—and watch what used to be difficult get easier.

Get More Zs

Sleep is good for you. Sleep is healing. It's not just physical rest... it's *soul* rest! You have to turn things over to God. Sometimes, that's hard! Start by giving Him the little stuff, and then work your way up to the big stuff. You don't have to wear all the care. Let it go! Leave your worries at the feet of the Lord. It's out of your hands!

Even if we know we need to rest, for a lot of us, it's still a constant battle. We refuse to give ourselves permission to enjoy it. We have to really fight to make time for ourselves to rest. Doubt creeps in: *Am I doing the right thing?* Worry: *Will they really be able to handle things without me?* Guilt: *I know everything will probably be okay... but am I just passing off my responsibility onto someone else?*

Stop resisting!

God needs your unique talents. He needs you at your best. He needs you to rest, or else you'll burn out and be of absolutely no use to anyone! Recognize that these lies are just the enemy trying to get you to second-guess yourself so that he can steal your rest.

There are a multitude of natural ways to start resting better. One is to stop working at a certain hour. Turn the phone off. Resist the urge to check that email. Instead, engage in something that takes your mind to a place that allows it to settle down. Do something you enjoy. Take a walk. Read a book. Watch a movie. Hang out with friends or family.

There are simple things, like putting lavender oil on your pillowcase, or taking a magnesium or melatonin supplement (make sure to check with your healthcare provider first) that can help your body de-stress. Buy sheets that make you want to lay down and a pillow that's comfortable. Try a routine that lets your mind know you're getting ready to settle in.

Try a bath or shower with some aromatherapy or bath salts. Dim the lights before brushing your teeth and read a devotional or a few pages of the Bible to settle your spirit. Say ten things you are thankful for today. Whatever it is that starts clueing your psyche into what's coming next—a good night's sleep.

Pamper Yourself (No One Else Will)

I guess I'm naturally a bit of a martyr. I usually don't sit down until everything is done, put away, and cleaned up. As soon as I know everyone else is okay, *then* I can relax (there's always just one more thing to do, so that almost never happens). At the same time, there's nothing wrong with accepting a little pampering. If someone else paints my toes or rubs my back, that makes me happy! It changes my mood and relaxes me. I'm a lot nicer when I'm relaxed.

Budget to get yourself a manicure or massage. Talk someone into that backrub. Sneak away for nine holes of golf. Support your local teenager and hire a babysitter to take your kids to the movies, the park or somewhere you're not.

If you're like me, you feel a little guilty being pampered. On my 40th birthday, David sent a car to pick up me and some friends to get our toes painted and our shoulders rubbed. Why did he include my friends? Because he knew I probably wouldn't go if it was just for me.

Recently, we were on vacation, and I told my husband that one thing I wanted to do that week was get a pedicure. There was never a good time to get in the car and go, so I just didn't. It wasn't a big deal to me. But I had the right circle around me to help me celebrate. My husband took me on the back of his motorcycle. I thought I was doing something for him, so I went along. Then, he dropped me off at the nail salon. I got chauffeur service, and he got all the points for taking care of me. All he had to do was drop me off and pick me up!

God knows that it's harder for some of us to rest, relax and take it easy. At night, when the world gets quiet, I can finally meditate on all my junk. Then, answers come flying to me in my sleep. I have to jump up and write stuff down (or lay awake, scared that I'm going to forget) and then try to go back to sleep.

That's *not* rest (but it *is* why I have my *Goal Getters Planner* next to my bed)!

> *"Let us labour therefore to enter into that rest, lest*
> *any man fall after the same example of unbelief."*
> —Hebrews 4:11 (KJV)

That's what the Sabbath is supposed to be: a day of (breathe in, breathe out) *rest!* A day to renew, revitalize, rejuvenate, and revive!

So today, I officially give you permission to pamper yourself. Doctor's orders. What does that mean? Schedule an hour for you. Or two. Maybe three. Why not make it four? Pamper yourself a little bit. That's what your body was built by the Creator of the Universe to do. He even modeled it Himself. On the seventh day, He rested. If even God rested, we can pamper ourselves with a little down time and enjoyment without feeling guilty, right?

> *You might not be where you want to be, but*
> *you're sure not where you used to be.*

Killing Guilt

I feel *guilty*. I'm at the office late (almost every day), and I feel guilty that I'm not with my kids or my husband. But when I spend time with my family, I feel guilty because I'm not working—even if it's my day off. Ironic, huh? I don't think I'm alone here. When I'm with the kids, I feel like I'm not paying enough attention to my husband. When I try to do something with just me and my better half, I feel like the kids are being left out. Whatever it is—dog, neighbors, the PTA, room mothers, my friends, or just an hour alone—I feel guilty about everyone else! How is that a win?

I remember when my husband and I first got married. We'd just bought a rehab project—ahem, a house. We were working day and night turning what we could afford into what would hopefully become the house of our dreams (at least, for that time). We were saving money by doing most of the work ourselves... until one night, oh man... I guess the chili from the night before disagreed with me.

I didn't want my new husband to know what was *really* happening behind closed doors. So I just told him I didn't feel great and went to lay down. About an hour later, he had to get something out of the bedroom. He was muttering under his breath—something about trying to handle a two-person job with just one person. He grumbled,

"Well, at least I'm not *lazy*..."

I was crushed! I'm *not* lazy! As a matter of fact, I'm just the opposite! I'm a Goal-Getter! I'm in it to win it! How could he say that about me? Why do we care so much what other people think, anyway? *Just because they think it doesn't make it true.* Time has a phenomenal way of revealing the truth. We have nothing to prove to them. I tried to get up and help him rehab the house, because guilt got the best of me. I helped him a little bit and then had to collapse back into bed.

A week or so later, we were in a hotel room at a conference. It was one of the first times we'd traveled together professionally as a married couple. We were figuring out our rhythms and suddenly, his was off. Both ends of his body alerted him at about the same time that something was desperately wrong. It was the same "chili effect" I'd experienced when he called me lazy. As I knocked on the locked bathroom door, asking if I could help, he was mortified and desperately asked me to stay out.

Later that night, as he was plastered to the sheets in the not-that-nice hotel-turned-sickroom, he profusely apologized over and over again.

"I am so sorry I called you lazy! I had no idea!"

My guilt about lying in bed had caused me to get up and try to help. But I guess I just infected him.

Guilt is a tool of the enemy! Guilt, somehow, actually *feels* right—justified. But our feelings are crazy, fickle creatures that are wrong as often as they're right! Here's where we kill guilt. I had to work myself up to this! Kill guilt! Kill guilt!

I know you might feel like you're laying down on the job by resting, but you're really doing the best thing for everyone concerned.

> *"Guilt: the gift that keeps on giving."*
> —Erma Bombeck

You Need a Hobby

In the U.S., we're so driven that we think, in order to be successful, we can't take any time off for a hobby. The fact is that it's hard to truly be successful without a hobby or some special interest. A hobby is a *reason* to break and engage with other people, doing something we enjoy—and that relieves stress! Let me ask you a couple of questions:

- Do you have a hobby?
- What is it?
- Can you do it with other people?
- When was the last time you did it?

If you don't have a hobby, what are three things you can imagine yourself doing to blow off some steam with other people?

You have to give yourself a break from the job. You need something that enables you to disconnect from the pressure. Activities allow your brain to do something entirely different. It's not just about fun—it's about rest! Change gears and go the distance. If you keep treating your body as if your life is a sprint, it'll be like driving from New York to Miami in *first gear!* Switch gears! Lower your RPMs. This secret will help you go further, faster.

GET REFUELED

A nun who worked for a local orphanage on the outskirts of town was on her way to an appointment when she ran out of gas. She started thanking God, immediately, when she realized that there was a gas station just one block away. She got in her steps and used the last of her energy to walk to the station to borrow a gas can.

The gas station attendant had the burden of telling her that he had loaned out his only fuel can. What was she going to do? The tired nun decided to walk back to her old station wagon and look for any kind of container that might possibly hold some gas. She found a new bedpan she was using to care for one of the orphans. Thankful that she hadn't taken it out of her car yet, she toted it to the fuel station, filled it with gasoline, and carried it back.

She poured the gas out of the bedpan into the tank, and realized that two men were watching her from across the street. One of the older gents on the bench leaned over to the other and said,

"I know that Jesus turned water into wine; but if that car starts, I'm going to church every Sunday for the rest of my life!"

Refueling might not look like you think it will. And it sure might not look like someone else expects. You have to find what works for *you!* (Hopefully, it doesn't involve a bedpan and a car with no gas! LOL.)

What Does It Take to Fill Your Tank?

Where I work, we don't have sick days. We hope that you don't have to waste one single day feeling unwell. Instead, we have personal days. If you call in sick, we will pray for you to feel better and for you to enjoy every moment!

Are you stuck trying to come up with ideas on how to refuel? Here are seven ideas to get you started!

#1 – Get a manicure and pedicure. Jesus got a pedicure (remember the alabaster flask?) and it doesn't get much more macho manly than Him! Ladies, if you don't like rubbing your hubby's feet, take him with you and do it together so it's not awkward for him (if he's never been before). Watch someone else do the work while you get the reward.

2 – Turn up the music. Do you remember how easy it used to be to get lost in the music? You didn't have a care in the world until your parents told you to turn it down. I'm giving you permission to *crank it!* (It is my last name, after all.) Dance in the living room like you're Tom Cruise from back in the day. Your kids will laugh at you and tell you that you look funny. That just makes it all the more fun!

#3 – Take a drive through a neighborhood you would love to live in. Pick out the house you like, the landscaping you want, and dream! If you don't like driving, take a walk. Sometimes, you just need to get out of the house. Breath in the fresh air and take note of all the beautiful things on your path.

#4 – Put the kids to bed early. Make tonight all about you. Light some candles and get into the tub. Or, if that's not your thing, head to the gym and let off a little steam. Don't feel bad about taking care of you. A healthy you builds a healthy life. A little alone time never hurt anybody.

> *"I have to be alone very often. I'd be quite happy if I spent from Saturday night until Monday morning alone in my apartment. That's how I refuel."*
> —Audrey Hepburn

#5 – Don't be overcome by stress when you're watching the news or current events. Your Father is God. All things will work out for your good. Period. Turn off the Negative Nancys and turn on something that makes you laugh. Then milk that laugh for all it's worth.

#6 – Don't feel guilty for being human. Allow yourself to cry. Allow yourself to fall down. If you never fall down, God can never pick you back up. Real men have feelings. Strong women aren't afraid to show theirs. I have a friend who says, "People would rather have a leader that's real than a leader that's always right."

#7 - Get to know what it takes to truly fill your tank and "*crank your tractor.*" This is like knowing your love language (and the love languages of the people around you).

Know Your Love Language

When we were first married, it seemed like I was always half-ticked-off at David: "Would you please just *help me*? I have *so* much to do! I'm working so hard and you're sitting on the couch!"

My love language is acts of service. If you *really* love me... then you'll take out the trash! I would gripe at him instead of filling up *his* "love tank" by saying stuff like, "Thank you for helping! It's so important to me! You do such a good job loading the dishwasher!" You see, my husband's love language is words of affirmation. He doesn't really feel loved or appreciated unless you say it out loud. So, when it comes to my life partner, I usually get more of what I brag on!

You can't fill up a car with water and expect it to run well. And a human can't drink gasoline and expect to feel great. You have to use the right fuel. If you haven't read the book, *The 5 Love Languages,* by Gary Chapman, it will change your life... for real! Everyone has a unique personality and a dominant love language. Everyone feels and expresses love differently.

The five love languages are:

- Words of Affirmation
- Quality Time
- Receiving Gifts
- Acts of Service
- Physical Touch

The bottom line is this... We can *never* refuel someone else's "love tank" the way *we* want to be loved. This was a big thing for me to learn; it changed the way I thought about a lot of things. We can't expect someone else to fill our tank if we don't know how to tell them how we hear and feel love.

Finding the right people to do life with is important; but so is *being* the right person for those in our lives!

GET REWARDS

> *"But as for you, be strong and do not give up, for your work will be <u>rewarded</u>."*
> —2 Chronicles 15:7

You've worked on how to stay committed (the part people don't usually get excited about)! I'm so proud of you! Now, let's look at *rewards* (The part we should be excited about but aren't for some reason!)

Why wouldn't we naturally do this? You have to celebrate where you are on the way to where you're going! Otherwise, it's going to seem too hard. It's going to be too tight. It's going to be too long, and you're going to want to give up. You have to party along the way—even if it's just a little bit: "Hey, we got $1,000 paid off on the credit card. Tonight, we go out to eat somewhere reasonable." Or maybe it's, "Guess what? I lost 10 pounds! Let's get that Starbucks drink we love tomorrow—A Trenta size!"

Congratulations: you have a reason to reward yourself, *right now! You're already a bigger success than you give yourself credit for!*

- You've written down your goals. You're already doing better than 97% of the world.
- Other people made resolutions/goals; but by writing them down, you're 42% more likely to accomplish yours.
- You're going to fully focus on your goals for 30 days and commit them to memory. Your focus will determine your direction, and your internal compass has been set toward success.
- You're *all-in*, fully committed to making your dreams reality!

There's so much more happening than you can see. It's time. It's time to plan some rewards and put them into your strategy. That's right: *reward plans*. Yes, we need to plan our rewards. Rewards Day for me means I'm out of the office. I get some fresh air. I get to touch a tree. I get to see something great! I get to feel the sun on my skin. This is pivotal!

> *"The plans of the diligent man, they lead to*
> <u>*profit*</u>. *As surely as haste leads to poverty."*
> —Proverbs 21:5

Here you are. You're planning, you're diligent, you're going after it. So it's time to profit a little bit from your efforts. God's going to give you the "desires of your heart" and make your plan succeed. I want to give you, right now… pay attention. I'm giving you permission to enjoy yourself. In the process of achieving what you want, let's pause to make sure that, in the other parts of our lives, we're becoming *who* we want to be!

> *What you GET by achieving your goals is not as important*
> *as what you BECOME by achieving your goals.*

I want you to celebrate where you are today. You might be thinking, "I'm working so hard. I'm eating no calories. I'm working out. I'm so deprived! That sounds like you're about ready to give up! Don't be that person who gives up on their dreams when what you really need is just some time off.

Little Rewards

Rewards are not always big. Sometimes, they're little rays of sunshine that brighten and lighten our day. I don't know what those rewards are for you. But they don't have to cost money.

Getting a shoulder rub from my husband is a reward for me. Not sure about him, but it's great for me. (When I'm done, it's a reward for him. Come on—it's how you build a healthy marriage #relationshipgoals.)

My husband and I work together. We once went one entire year working back-to-back, seven-day work weeks. But we knew that was coming, so we planned a couple of times for a few days off. Knowing that those days off were coming gave me what I needed to hold on. Eight months into this 12-month plan, I began to see the light at the end of the tunnel. I kept reminding myself that it was all coming to an end—that a reward day was near. I *leaned* on that day. I *dreamed about* that day. That's what got me through!

If you've been dedicated, I want you to celebrate winning the small battles on the way to winning the war. Celebrate each battle. Celebrate each victory. Where are you going, and where can you plan a celebration along the way? Planning little rewards will keep you happy. It will keep you excited and moving in the right direction.

The point is this: you have to *plan them*.

Decide what a victory looks like for you and...

Eat the Cake

Work hard, exercise, eat healthy, take time to rest, love God, love your family, and attend church. Take care of business! But, once in a while, it's okay to…

- Eat the cake!
- Binge on Netflix!
- Sleep all day!
- Turn off your work phone!
- Have a movie marathon!
- Order the appetizer, the meal *and* the dessert!

Being steady and faithful most of the time makes it possible for us to indulge once in a while without beating ourselves up and feeling guilty. After all, what we do consistently, every day, is different from what we do occasionally.

Once in a while, relax and *enjoy!* It will help you appreciate this wonderful life God has given you!

> *"Goals are the fuel in the furnace of achievement."*
> —Brian Tracy

Bonus:
GET TIPS, TRICKS, AND HACKS

GET ROUTINE: HACKS TO GET YOU THERE ON AUTOPILOT

The secret of life lies in your daily routine—the discipline, the little tweaks that lead to giant peaks.

It isn't what you do every once in a while; it's what you do consistently that makes all the difference.

Back in my corporate days, my husband used to brag on me. I was "The Closer." I was the person who could make the deal! But to tell you the truth, I wasn't really that good of a sales person. Put me in a room full of people, and I'm actually kind of shy. So how did I become so good at sales? (I'll tell you the secret…)

Devise a daily routine and stick to it.

Starting a business? In sales? Consistently make 20 cold calls, every day, whether you feel like it or not. That's the hard part! You're gonna get a lot of "nos". You'll have to deal with a lot of rejection. But in the end, it will usually pay off...*big time!*

So, what are some things you can build into your routine to make reaching your goals a little easier?

Guard Your Productivity

Do you ever talk to people, only to have them give more focus to their phone, texts, and emails than to you? In a society full of distractions, where phones are extensions of our arms and our notifications come in all types of sounds, vibrations, and flashes, it's a great compliment to have someone's total focus. Imagine what results we might achieve if our undistracted focus was applied toward our goal!

Jesus had a busy speaking schedule. People were constantly asking Him to solve all their problems. He always had crowds around Him, following Him everywhere He went. Despite great demands on His time, He guarded His productivity by taking the time to get away from people. During those times, He prayed and reconnected to God.

Do you take time to get away and think in a distraction-free environment? Make the time. Schedule it! Jesus was committed to His purpose. He stayed focused and maintained boundaries in order to keep His momentum towards His goal.

Here's some things that work for me:

- Mornings are best. I have to do it before my brain is bombarded by the day's demands. My creativity is dumbed down by email if I read it first thing in the morning.
- Being busy isn't enough. We need to ask, "What am I busy *with*?" It's a self-defeating lie to think that others can't get along without us!
- When I'm trying to think creatively, I use a pad and pen instead of electronics. Think outside the box! Scribble down whatever drops into your mind!
- God will drop amazing solutions and ideas into your mind if you'll take the time to be quiet and allow Him the opportunity.
- Have you ever noticed that we tend to get the things done that are the most important to us—or just plain easy?

GET A Winning Routine (Check!)

I always have a "to-do" list. I know—there are many ways to keep track. There are really cool apps like Trello, Basecamp, Evernote, Asana and so many more that can follow your work in progress. Or there's good, old-fashioned paper! (Seriously, having it in my *Goal Getters Planner* keeps it before my eyes.)

I like to list the stuff I want to accomplish in categories: *today, tomorrow, this week, this month,* or *this year.* Making a list and following it will help you get where you want to go.

Checking off a task (no matter how small) always makes me feel happy! It's those *little wins* that give us the motivation to move on to the next thing on our list. If cleaning the whole house seems a bit daunting, just divide it into smaller tasks:

Today I will:
Wash the sheets. (Check)
Mow the lawn. (Check)

And stop feeling guilty about the stuff you don't get done. I know I do that. Regret and guilt will try to take yesterday's shortcomings and make them today's problems. Today is a *new day!* It's the little foxes that spoil the vine! Get those foxes of regret out of the field (revisit the "Kill Guilt" section above if you're still getting stuck in this rut)!

> *"I hate housework! You make the beds, you do the dishes and six months later you have to start all over again."*
> —Joan Rivers

Remember, success is simply getting up one more time than you fall down!

This morning, you got up—*check!* You're on the right track! Always be improving, creating a list, and checking it off—making progress… and celebrate the little wins along the way!

You've made a commitment and you've written it down. At the end of the year, I want to hear where you are. I'm proud of you for what you're doing. You're going to make it to your goal. It's going to happen! God's given you the strength. He put that desire inside of your heart, and you're going to go all the way! You're going to make it through to the end!

> *"Faith is taking the first step even when*
> *you don't see the whole staircase."*
> —Martin Luther King, Jr.

6 Steps to GETTING a Happy Routine

#1: Make it routine to: Cheer up your coworkers
If the people around you are enjoying their day, it'll be a lot easier for you to enjoy yours. The best way to brighten someone's day is to affirm them with positive statements. This costs you nothing! Everyone wants to feel accepted; so make it your goal to compliment someone today.

#2: Make it routine to: Stay focused for one hour at a time
It's a little goal with a big payoff. You'll be surprised how much you can get done if you don't allow yourself to be interrupted for one hour. Studies have proven that it takes 15 minutes to get

back on track after an interruption. "Productive-ness" leads to happiness—especially for a Goal Getter.

Have a 60-second productivity routine to start your hour:

- Close your email.
- Put your phone on silent.
- Shut your door.
- Put a Post-it Note on your door letting people know you are unavailable until _____.

#3: Make it routine to: Pay Active Attention

Whatever you do, do well. For when you go to the grave,
there will be no work or planning or knowledge or wisdom.
—Ecclesiastes 9:10 (NLT)

Over time, making a conscious effort to pay active attention will make your mind twice as sharp. Oftentimes, I listen to podcasts on 1.5 speed. Then, I repeat what they're saying so my mind doesn't wander off. This helps me stay focused on the task at hand.

#4: Make it routine to: Drink loads of water

Although coffee is the Christian's drug of choice (LOL), water is the secret to sustained energy. While it's easy to stop by QuikTrip and load up on soda, caffeine is only able to make you feel alert for a short time. Next time you need a quick pick-me-up, try chugging two glasses of water.

Up to 60% of the human body is water. The brain is composed of 70% water. Water is the easiest way to keep your mind alert and your body refreshed. And you can't beat the price! (Plus, the extra couple of trips to the bathroom will help you get in some extra steps. LOL.)

#5: Make it routine to: Celebrate you!
You need to hear it again: when you complete the task, finish the project, or make the sale, make a big deal out of it. Take yourself to lunch. Do something you've wanted to do. Give thanks.

#6: Make it routine to: Organize your workspace
Clean your office (and desk). Sharpen your pencil. Clear out your inbox. Organize your desktop. If you keep everything in order, you'll be more productive.

One last thing—make it routine to: Start right now!

There's truly no time like the present. Remember the value of execution that we talked about? Do each of these six little things, and I promise: you are going to feel more in charge of your life (and the people around you are going to be shocked).

GET USED TO FOLLOWING THE FAVOR

Back in 2007, we were vacationing in Destin, Florida. I can remember David saying, "We're gonna spend years of our lives on white sandy beaches!" I thought, U*h, okay... but what are you talking about? We live in landlocked Missouri! The only beach there is made of river rock, on the banks of the muddy Mississippi.*

We always thought we'd have a church in South Florida someday. But we had no idea exactly where we'd end up. However, when you're living in rewards, sometimes you just have to follow the favor.

We had some friends who moved to West Palm Beach and asked us, "What would it take to get a church down here?" First, we'd have to be on TV. So our friends decided they'd go ahead and pay for that— for *three years! Wow!*

Florida had always been on our goals list. Now, God had us in just the right place to set us up in a coastal city we'd never even been to before. On our first visit, our friends showed us their office space. One of our team members called me from St. Louis and said, "Hey, we're going on TV in West Palm Beach. Are you sure you want to list a St. Louis address for a Florida broadcast?"

Great point! I said, "Okay, I'm going upstairs to tour our friend's new office. Then I'll stop by the post office and get us a Florida post office box. I'll call you back in an hour." We toured their offices: a beautiful penthouse space in one of the most exclusive office buildings in downtown West Palm Beach, with a fabulous view of the water. When we finished the tour, our friends said, "You know what? We've got way too much space—more than we can use. Would you guys like some office space here, for *free*?"

Uhhhh… Yes!

Only an hour earlier, we'd needed a Florida address. Now, we didn't just have an address—we had an entire office— a premium, downtown, penthouse office—for *free!*

When we got downstairs, I called the team back and said, "Sorry, we don't have a post office box—we've got a new office! And here's the address, 777 Flagler. All sevens! God's favor caused us to hit the jackpot! God provided us with free office space and free television time! (Woohoo!) That was the beginning of our ministry in West Palm Beach. Now, with two church campuses in Florida, we travel back and forth to preach and spend a lot of time on those white sandy beaches (just like my husband had on his goals list).

When the door of opportunity opens, follow it.

Don't spend your time trying to beat down doors that won't budge. *"No" isn't always a bad word. Sometimes, it's a reroute to a better "yes."* So don't ignore the open doors while trying to kick in the closed ones. It's called following the favor. You'll encounter people who prefer you for the job over everyone else, even though your resume isn't as good. You'll get upgrades and preferential treatment you didn't earn. The words "I don't know why I'm doing this, but…" will be said to you. Just accept the grace. It's called favor!

God is really into giving you the desires of your heart—sweet *rewards!* And sometimes, the reward—even the house near the beach—can be an open door to the next level in life that you would never have had access to if you hadn't followed the favor!

GET OUT OF THE RUT: WHAT TO DO WHEN YOU FEEL STUCK

Sometimes, we think we can't get where we'd love to go because, well, you just can't get *there* from *here*. Sometimes, it seems like we were cruising along just fine; then, suddenly, our wheels are turning as fast as we can move them and nothing is happening but a bunch of mud flying and messing everything up. God isn't shocked by where you are today. His plan isn't thrown off because of a failed job, rocky marriage, leadership gap, lack of credit, or anything else. In fact, you're right where you need to be to get where you're going. God has the directions to where you are called to go. "I know the *plans* I have for you." That's what God Himself said in Jeremiah 29. Then, He let us know they aren't crummy, second-rate, plan-B-type plans.

No! They are for a *good future!*

Have you ever filled out a bank loan? It's a stupid amount of information and paperwork. Have you ever done all that work and gotten turned down? It's so discouraging. Can you imagine doing all of that work for 100 different banks and getting turned down 100 different times? Would you keep going? What if you got turned down 200 times? Would you quit?

Thank God, Howard Schultz didn't get stuck where he started! Who's Howard? Only a guy who got turned down for a loan 242 times. But on try 243, he was able to start Starbucks (without which it is entirely possible I would be a grouchier person). Good thing that rut didn't stop him! When we are faithful over whatever little we have, now (where we are starting), God finds a way to bless it and help us to rule over more.

> *"May he give you the desire of your heart*
> *and make all your plans succeed."*
> —Psalm 20:4

Don't Get Stuck Where You Started

Your destination isn't dependent on your origination.

You don't hear, "You can't get there from here" in today's society. You might have a layover. It might not be a direct flight. It might require a plane, train, boat and automobile. But you can get *anywhere* from here—and I don't just mean geographically.

Don't let a little thing like…

- your literal location ("I live in wrong zip code, on wrong side of town, nobody from here ever went anywhere...")
- your perceived life location ("I never finished college, I had children young, I made a mistake when I was younger so it's over for me...")
- or your self-location ("I'm the wrong gender, ethnicity, age, IQ, body type...")

...keep you from dreaming big, GETting your dreams, and making your doubters eat it. You can spin your wheels at a pity party all day long, but no one will see it except you. Those parties aren't well attended. And whatever you do, never blame the rut of "lack of experience." All of us were born with that. If you don't manage a single person at work outside of yourself, manage yourself like you would someone else. Show everyone you know how to be the boss, because you are effectively the boss of you!

Don't get stuck where you start. God's plans are way bigger than you can imagine!

Get Rid of the Suckers

Exclusion is the process of adding to your life by subtraction.

Wait a minute... does that make mathematical sense? Add to your life by subtracting? Yep—bad math, but great life practice. See if this rings a bell...

You wake up to your Saturday morning "To-Do" list. You have to hit your "Honey-Do" list, grocery shop, do laundry, cut the grass, clean the house, and so much more. But first… you're going to check your Facebook really fast. (Yeah, right.) An hour later, you look up and you're still on your computer.

You had to Twitter your Facebook and Facebook your Instagram. Then, you had to read a gazillion forwarded emails and cute stories. They touched you so much that you shed a tear and felt compelled to share them on Facebook because you didn't want anybody to miss them. Another hour is gone.

(Did you know that Twitter and Facebook are merging? They're going to call it "Twit-Face." This is about how I feel at the end of that long hour—a.k.a., a time-waster.)

How does this happen? These are things that suck energy, time, and emotion out of our lives. How can we identify them in order to eliminate them? In order to go to the next level and get our 10,000 hours of focus on the talents we want to develop, we need to subtract certain things from our lives so we can grow and multiply in the areas in which God wants to grow us.

This is one of the greatest Goal-Getting hacks in the whole book. I hope you are highlighting this one.

> *"To win the contest you must deny yourselves many things that would keep you from doing your best."*
> —1 Corinthians 9:25 (TLB)

Can't Take 'Em with You

Sometimes, those things we're supposed to exclude, change, and deny aren't just things—but certain people. The people we hang around are the people we're going to become like.

> *"Do not be misled: 'Bad company corrupts good character.'"*
> —1 Corinthians 15:33 (NIV)

If we're going to progress in life, we should assess the time-suckers, emotion-suckers, drama-mongers, troublemakers, and those who want to make their bad decisions our problem. Have you ever noticed that sometimes, the people who liked you before you made it don't like you so much once they see how blessed you are? Remember, that we have friends for a *reason* and friends for a *season*. Not everyone who's been with us thus far will go with us the entire distance! "But God... I *like* these people!" I whined in my whiniest voice. Have you ever said that?

God is calling you to go to the next level; but you can't climb a ladder with somebody else on your back.

Sometimes, we're afraid and think, "But God, they're my friends. I'm not going to have anybody else." God is whispering, "If you would just climb the ladder, I have new mentors, new friends, and a new circle of friends to speak into your life up here. Just be willing to follow My plan. If you really like those people… you're gonna *love* the people I have to take you to the next level!"

God has a calling on your life. Follow it. Trust Him. Be willing to give up the things that are holding you back. You'll be able to run so much faster without all that extra weight.

It only gets better! Know that *promotion* comes from heaven:

- Better *pay!*
- Better *relationships!*
- Better *peace!*
- Better *opportunity!*
- Better *life!*

Don't let the people who won't celebrate your victories keep you down!

Get Bolder in Your Prayer Time

Is it okay to pray for success?

Absolutely… *yes!* If we aren't praying for success, what's the alternative? Are we going to pray for God to make us fail? When our success honors God and helps people, there's nothing selfish about it.

> *"And God can give you more blessings than you need.*
> *Then you will always have plenty of everything—*
> *enough to give to every good work."*
> —2 Corinthians 9:8 (NCV)

Let's start to pray specifically about what we want to see happen. That's success defined!

I remember when we first decided to go on ABC almost 20 years ago. We envisioned having a time slot somewhere near Joel Osteen's Sunday morning program. We actually cut the TV listings out of the newspaper (remember those?), circled the time in red, and taped it to our refrigerator (the beginning of my Post-it Note theory). Every time we got hungry (which was quite often), we would remember to *pray* expressly over that time slot. Since we were praying for a particular outcome, it was easy to recognize our success when that exact time slot became available and was offered to us, first. Success is our testimony!

If our idea of success is easily attainable, then it's probably not God's.

He enjoys getting *all* the credit. That's why He usually gives us dreams that are *way too big* for us to possibly accomplish on our own. This is exactly why I encourage you to dream big in your goal-setting!

If our life achievements continue to glorify God, I'm sure He's totally okay with us praying for more success!

Get Out of the Unworthy Rut

Most of the time, I don't feel worthy of getting to do what I do. *Why would God pick somebody like me? He should pick someone older, wiser, more educated: someone better…someone more WORTHY.* Do you ever feel small and insignificant, like you aren't making a difference? Do you feel like you've gotten chances in life that you didn't deserve, and may have wasted?

Am I reading your mail… or just mine?

Everybody screws up. Everybody makes mistakes. Everybody sins. It doesn't matter if someone else looks more qualified than you. *God doesn't choose us based on our worthiness. He chooses us based on our willingness… because none of us are worthy.*

The question is, are you willing to go? Are you willing to face what looks like opposition (but what God knows is actually an opportunity)? If your answer is yes, get ready! God is so wild! What He will ask will be unusual. How He asks can be interesting. His timing is mind-boggling. His faith in us is unimaginable!

I don't think you're reading this by accident. It's very intentional that we're not ending this Goal-Getting journey with an exercise—something technical, or a project. I'm leaving you with encouragement and assurance. I understand that your dreams got kind of wild here. But so did a childless Abraham when he looked at the stars when he was *well* past middle age, when he believed that his descendants would outnumber those very stars. And it happened!

I'm here to assure you that the dreams and desires you prayed about, wrote down, meditated on, visualized, and are executing are coming your way—whether you are "worthy" or not.

Want to Be Successful?

If you're like me, you want it to happen before 5 o'clock today. Or, if you're really patient, tomorrow will be fine. We always want to take the express elevator to the top. We want to rush our success. We want it *now!* Don't get me wrong: many times we do experience accelerated favor from God. But more often than not, reaching a goal or achieving success is more of a *process*.

Maybe you've heard the story about the young boy who tried to help a butterfly escape from its cocoon by cutting the cocoon away. Initially, it sounded like he was trying to be of assistance. Fortunately, he was stopped by his father, who was able to explain the process to him. You see, it's the struggle of getting out of the cocoon that strengthens the butterfly's wings and enables it to reach its full potential and fly. Success is a process! Remember the water hyacinth as you close this book.

Our *talent* may take us somewhere fast, but only our *character* has the ability to keep us there.

We should take full advantage of the process of achieving success to develop and strengthen our character. It's not just what we are achieving, but who we are becoming during the Goal-Getting process. The person you are in five years is going to have so much to say to the "you" of today!

Now, close the book, put your chin up (or the crown slips my kings and queens), and go *get* what you have coming to you!

Blessings!